Black Hole To Life

Black Hole To Life

A True Story

Cindy Leopard

iUniverse, Inc.
New York Bloomington

Black Hole To Life
A True Story

iUniverse books may be ordered through booksellers or by contacting:

iUniverse
1663 Liberty Drive
Bloomington, IN 47403
www.iuniverse.com
1-800-Authors (1-800-288-4677)

Because of the dynamic nature of the Internet, any Web addresses or links contained in this book may have changed since publication and may no longer be valid.

ISBN: 978-1-4401-6750-8 (sc)
ISBN: 978-1-4401-6749-2 (ebk)

Printed in the United States of America

iUniverse rev. date: 10/6/2009

DEDICATION

This book is dedicated to the people in my life who are
responsible for my being alive today and loving
life once again:

My faithful and loving God, who has taught me
the meaning of the term "Unshakable Faith,"
my beautiful and loving children, Heather and Benjamin
Johnson,
who gave me the will and strength to not leave them,
my loving parents, Buddy and Alice, who quickly became
my caretakers and taught me the love of what a
mom and dad can be, my wonderful sister and brother,
Sharon and Lance, who gave me hope and their time
for whatever I needed, my new Pastor Schuyler
Peterson and my new church family
At Ft. Johnson Baptist Church.
My fabulous Doctors who have treated me like a person
they truly care about, Dr. Fred Pooser and Dr. Joseph Zealberg
and
all of the caregivers that took me into their care, and took great
care of me.

Now my true friends for life, I have come to the conclusion
that the only way to list them is in the order of the
amount of years that I have known them.

They are all so important to me, it would never
be fair to list them in any other way, for they are
all so dear to me and have helped me in so many ways.
Rosemarie Crombie (Rosie), Marie Mizzell,
Shirley Shannon (Sam), Linda Evans and Barry Waldrop.

If I lived for a thousand years, I would never be able
to thank you all enough for everything, I will love
you all forever and God Bless you all.

Contents

PROLOGUE

Yes, I was living the perfect life! I was having the time of my life. I was healthy, my children and my family were all doing great and I was in love. I had never been this happy in my entire life until it all turned upside down in a matter of a minute. The man I loved more than any other man in my life left me very unexpectedly which put me in a state of shock. The shock led to catatonic depression, severe panic, severe anxiety, suicidal ideations and failure to thrive. I want to tell my story so that it may help others that find themselves with the same illnesses and for the caregivers taking care of them. I have now been there where they are and have found my way back to life. This has been a journey of wellness that seemed impossible to me at the time, but with very hard work and finding faith, strength, courage and power; I am now recovering and feel that my story can help others.

As I take on the task of writing a book, please understand a few things about me. Firstly, I have never been a writer and this is the last thing in this world I ever planned to do, but I feel that this book about my illness has to be told. Secondly, this book is a true story and I am using the real names of the people in the book that I have written permission to use. They are the people in my life that went through this ordeal with me and I would not be here today without them. Thirdly, the proceeds of the book will go to two things. I want to pay my parents back the money they had to spend on my care. They had to take out a mortgage on their home that I would like to pay back. I also want to pay all of my medical bills that have occurred since I lost my medical insurance four weeks after my illness began. I would then like to give money to a charity which is "*The Mental Health Association of Charleston, South Carolina.*" I would love to give all the money to charity, but I feel that my family, hospitals and doctors deserve to be paid. They all took such great care of me during these times and believe me I was hospitalized many, many times with no money to pay for these visits.

As I begin this book, I realize that I must begin with my life before I got sick or you will never understand that this kind of illness can happen to anyone, even a very happy person who has always lived a happy life and never had any signs of any mental illness before. It is very important that you the reader understand why I am taking on this task and letting my life during this illness be known. Please understand that I am using journals at times to help me remember things through this illness, for I do not remember a lot due to medications or just being too sick. I am very thankful now that I did write in a journal or I would not be able to share this story with you. I want everyone that reads this book to understand that this is not an illness to be ashamed of. That is not the way to ever heal from this kind of illness. Your family and your friends will become your lifelines, and yes you will need them to talk to.

I am a professional in the medical field as a Registered Nurse and have worked in a lot of the hospitals in the area that I live, which is Charleston, South Carolina. Through my faith, courage, and self-confidence that I have learned through this process, I want everyone to know that one day I will be back again to my profession. But I will not go back until I know that I am a safe and competent nurse again. It will not be a day before. This is not an illness that I will carry for the rest of my life, but it is an illness that will take time for me to overcome. This is ok because I know that I will be my true self again.

The illness that I went through can affect every aspect of your life and leave you with fears that are unfathomable to ever begin to describe, for example; to just be able to walk into a public place which I have done all my life, is now something that I can not do yet due to panic. But with unshakable faith, hard work and lots of strength, I know that I will. Now I am going to try my best to take you all to the place where I was, so that it can help you or others to understand how they can help someone in this situation. It is a very misunderstood illness and an illness that is very tricky to try to deal with by your family, loved ones and friends.

I am including "*Notes*" pages after a few of the chapters to help the reader who is sick and the caregiver. This would have been a great help to my mom with keeping up with my medications (especially the ones that made me so sick so that we would make sure I was never prescribed those again), my doctors with phone numbers and appointment dates, foods I could eat and the ones that made me sick, or to just make notes for yourself for whatever you need to remember. It is very important to keep up with all of this information at all times.

I am going to give it my best and open my heart and soul to you and the world to try to help others, *for my purpose on this earth is to help others!*

CHAPTER ONE

My Life
(Before)

I

When I start to talk about my life before my illness began, I guess I will start at the beginning which is my birth. I was born on July 15, 1959 to the two coolest parents in the whole world. They were very young when they met and had all three of us children by the time my mom was 19 years old. I have always thought this was pretty neat, because they kind of got to grow up with us (well I should add, what growing up we did). As I remember my childhood I have very happy memories, because we always had so much fun.

My mom and dad spent a lot of time at the Folly Beach Pier dancing the Folly Beach Shag, so us kids got to play at the amusement park all the time. We also spent a lot of time at the pier, got autographs of all kinds of cool old time musicians like Jerry Lee Lewis. So we all learned how to dance the shag by the time we could walk. I can remember my sister and me practicing in front of the picture window in the living room, just laughing and having a great time. It was devastating to us all when the pier burned down in the 80's, for it was like our second home. My mom went into labor with Sharon after dancing one night on that pier and I truly believe I was conceived somewhere around that ocean. I am the only Cancer in the group, and what a Cancer I am. I didn't know this then, but I sure would later as I grew up and became an adult.

My dad worked at this great place called *Charleston Oil Company* and I call it great because we kids had a ball there too. There was a huge warehouse full of cases of Quaker State Motor Oil and we used to climb all over them and hide from each other. We loved going to work with him, everyone there was great and so good to us. My dad had this really cool secretary and she would baby-sit for us at times. Well talk about fun, she would do all kinds of crazy things with us. She would come over and drink beer and smoke, but of course we never told mom and dad about that (yeah like they didn't know anyway), but we were a little older then, so it was ok. They knew we were safe with her and she loved us, little did we know at the time that she would stay in our lives forever. My mom was a stay at home mom so we always had her there while dad was working and yes he worked long and hard hours, I guess he had to if he was going to feed five people. Laughter was always around us all the time and it was great.

My school years were fun and I was a pretty good student. I always made good grades and made a lot of friends, some I would keep in my life forever. We lived in a great neighborhood and went to school with all of our neighbors and had a great time after school. We came home and mom always had us a great snack, we did our homework and then hit the streets with our friends. We all hung out together, but of course life was so different back then. Parents didn't have to worry about their kids getting kidnapped and all that bad stuff like they do today and kids in the same neighborhood do not all go to the same schools anymore. Therefore; they have nobody to hang out with these days.

II

Middle school was fun, that's when I started my crush on the guy down the street, I was about 14 and he was 15. He was my brother's best friend, so I kind of had to fight to be noticed, but I was and oh he was hot. We were too young for anything to go into something different, so we just ended up remaining friends, which was great. So the dating began and I quickly realized that I really liked boys a lot.

Around this time was when we started going to great places for the weekends on family outings. My dad's bosses owned great plantation homes like Medway Plantation and Anchorage Plantation. First came Medway Plantation and these were some of the best times of my life, we would take our friends with us and have a ball. Of course mom and dad didn't know half the things we were doing, like sneaking out in the middle of the night, smoking cigarettes and sometimes a beer or two. I could never understand how they never noticed how so many of these things were missing. My mom must have thought she smoked three packs of cigarettes a day, but of course never said anything. So Sharon and I would take out girlfriends, Lance would take his guy friends and of course the fun would just never stop.

Then Anchorage Plantation came in to play, Sharon and I and our friends would stay at the boathouse at Anchorage Plantation and of course our boyfriends would sneak out there after mom and dad would go to sleep. I remember us girls skinny dipping in the enclosed heated pool and having a ball, little did we know the boys were watching the whole time, this we would find out later in life. This place was on the water so we had access to the boats and all. We were a little older now, so the first thing we found out was how to get in to the liquor cabinet on the dock, the lock was pretty pathetic. Damn those were the days of our lives.

III

The next guy I dated lasted a long time through high school and this is when I really, really began to like boys a lot, he was great and we had a great time together. Actually I kind of stole him from my best childhood friend who lived down the street from me. She called me and told me to come down and meet her new boyfriend and I ended up taking him home with me. I apologized to her many times, but I don't think she ever really forgave me. But what can I say, he went with me. He lived around the corner from my grandparents, so of course I stayed at grandma's house every weekend to see him more. He was a few years older than me. He was out of school and working and I had just started driving a car. This was the first time I think I really loved a guy, so I guess you could say he was my first love. They had a guest house down by the water and I was allowed to stay there, but he had to stay at his house after 11:00 p.m. Yeah (that worked). His parents also went to sleep at night, so guess what? I still think of him sometimes and wonder where he is and wish him the best. As the saying goes, you never forget your first love. I know for sure I will never forget mine.

IV

Through my high school years is when I started seeing a lot of changes in my family and they were not good things. I began to notice that my father was an alcoholic and quickly began to realize why we always had so much fun. Have you ever heard the phrase "*We put the fun in dysfunctional,*" well we did! Sharon and Lance were choosing that same partying path to go down but I was not. I quickly realized that was not the life for me, so we all became separated at this time. They went their way and I went mine. I did not like our life at home anymore; the fun had gone away and would not come back for many years to come. Things were getting totally out of control at home, I was finding myself waiting up for my dad to get home at night and be safe and I knew my mom was doing the same. Sometimes I would sit in the hallway in the dark and just cry for her and all of us. My first love and I had broken up after two years and so I started looking for a way out.

This is when I would meet my first husband, whom I had great feelings for but I also knew I never loved. I was only 17 years old, so I quit school and got my GED and went to work for an Attorney down town on Broad Street. I was married then, but it would not last but about a year. But I was free and away from home. I have always felt bad for hurting him for it was kind of like I used him to get out of the house. I did not realize that at the time, but I did know it later and am very fortunate that we remained friends to this day and I am still close to his family. His family would really come back to my life in about 30 years in an incredible way - you will see.

Now, it was the late 70s and I was on my own, had a great duplex by myself and worked hard for an attorney that was great. This is where I met Rosie, wow were the three of us a team, we were busy but always had time for fun and great times. Rosie and I became life long friends and shared all of our thoughts and feelings with each other. She was divorced too so we had a lot in common, we always found the wrong men. Now I moved into this great apartment on Wentworth Street on the third floor of this old house and it was the coolest place. There was another apartment on the other side, where this guy lived and we used to share electricity when one of us could not pay our bills (what a set up that was). I lived there for awhile, but of course ended up back on James Island after about a year or so. Rosie also lived on James Island so we always hung out together after work and went to happy hour. She introduced me to tomato soup with milk in it and it was the greatest remedy to feel better the next day. Yeah Rosie!

Now it was the 1980s and I was still working for the same attorney and this is when I met my second husband, Billy Johnson. He was a Folly Beach boy and had been best friends with my cousin. I had never met him before with Harry but, it is a small world. I met Billy at a funeral and decided I would keep him and I did. Our first date was on the night when we found out who shot JR on *Dallas*, so of course we ended up at the beach at his best friend's house and we all watched *Dallas*. We had a great time and ended up dating and falling in love. To this day, I still think he liked his dog (Nikki) better than me, but it worked. So I began to meet Billy's friends and this is how Marie and Johnny Mizzell and Bonnie Mizzell came into my life. Marie was Billy's best friend's sister so of course we ended up there first. They had three small children and we hung out with them a lot. Marie, Bonnie and I quickly became great friends and would end up being friends for life.

V

Billy proposed in the backyard of my parent's house and of course I said yes. We got married in my grandmother's backyard down by the marsh in Byrnes Down and it was a wonderful day. This was in 1981 and life would soon begin to get very wonderful and very busy. We lived on the beach for a little while and this is when I would ask God for something for the first time in my life. I had always thanked him for everything he had ever given me, but now I asked him for something. I asked him to bless me with a beautiful, healthy baby girl one night in the middle of the night. I woke up and realized that if I made a baby at that time, she could possibly be born on my birthday. Well it worked and three weeks later I found out I was pregnant with my first child. This was the first most exciting day of my life, for I could not wait to be a mother and now my wish was going to come true. My due date was my birthday, but you will have to wait to see if this happens.

We then moved into a house right down the street from Marie and Johnny in Riverland Terrace and we loved it. We had a huge yard, a big garden every summer and great neighbors, everything you would ever want. We would end up staying there for about seven years, so you know it had to be great. We settled in and I just got bigger and bigger every day, boy was I huge pregnant. I felt great throughout the entire pregnancy, but it just wouldn't go by fast enough. We had the nursery all ready and everything we needed, so we just had to wait. I had quit working at this time, so I spent a lot of time with Marie because she was also a stay at home mom. I got some great lessons on raising children from mom and her and would end up getting many more for many years to come. I think my mom was waiting for this baby to come as much as I was, for it was her first grandchild and I thought at times that she thought it was going to be hers. She also set up a nursery at her house and I remember having this gut feeling that this baby was going to be spoiled rotten to the core; little did I know just how much. My best friend from high school now had two children and another on the way, so she could not wait either.

VI

Well the day finally came and I went into labor on July 10, 1982. Well everyone always told me having a baby hurt, but after 26 hours of labor I can tell you that having a baby really does hurt. I finally had a c-section (after 26 hours) and finally my beautiful, healthy daughter that I had asked God for was born on July 11, 1982 and weighed in at 7lbs. 11oz. (Remember this date for you will see it again). When I woke up from surgery all I could see was my mom, sister, mother in law, and both grandmothers asking me what I was going to name her. All I knew was that she was going to be Heather and then I had to name her after all of these other family members. So she ended up being "Heather Faye Antley Johnson." I covered almost everyone that other children had not been named after already and then I started thinking how this tiny little baby was ever going to ever carry this huge name. The first time I saw her, I could not believe my eyes. She was so beautiful and smelled so sweet that I started crying and would not stop for weeks. Every time I touched her it was like a miracle that she was mine, yes I would share her but she was mine.

I will never forget the first time her father picked her up and held her, I knew at that time that she would always be a daddy's girl and boy was I right. She is the still the apple of his eyes and always will be. I have always said that if I ever did anything right it was picking the father of my children, that I never could have done better. My mom really wanted her so much, she would come over when we were taking our nap, come in the back door and get Heather, her bottles, diapers and take her to her house. I would wake up and go into her room and she would be gone again. I would call Billy and tell him to go get Heather on his way home from work and bring her home, so he would. My mom would always say, "Oh she can just stay the night," but Billy would have to say no, she has to go home to Cindy, but she can come back over tomorrow. So Heather started growing up and then she turned one year old.

This is when I went through one of the worst times of my life, my best friend was murdered. She was missing for about two to three months and was finally found in the woods about 50 miles from home. She had just had her third child and was so happy in her life. I will never understand how this could have happened to one of the best people in the world, but I guess God's plan was that he needed a beautiful angel and he sure did get one. I miss her still to this day and I will never forget her. I had Heather's first birthday pictures made in a dress that my friend had given her and every time I look at it, I celebrate her life on this earth and pray that she is happy in Heaven.

So Heather began growing up and becoming very independent. She was born that way and would be the rest of her life. There are two really cute stories I want to tell you about her so that you will understand her personality. The first was when she was about 3-4 years old and was in the bathtub. I was washing her hair and she asked me "Mama when am I going to get boobies?" Well I answered her that around the time she went to high school she would probably begin to grow some. Her response to me was "That's good mama, so when you go to high school maybe you will grow some too." Well the only thing that saved her from being drowned that night was the fact that I was laughing so hard, I didn't think about it till later. The second was when her father broke both of his ankles at work one day. When I went to pick her up from school I told her we had to take good care of daddy because he broke both of his feet at work and could not work, so we really had to do a lot for him. So we got home and she ran into the living room and there was Billy lying on the couch with casts on both of his feet. She immediately said "Look mama daddy got his feet back, he didn't break them." We laughed so hard when we realized she thought that he had broken them both off completely. She was a trip and still is.

VII

Now came the time for me to ask God for my second gift that I wished for and that was a beautiful, healthy baby boy. Well again I started thinking that if I got pregnant right then I would have a baby on Heather's birthday, so I called Billy at work made him come home for lunch to make a baby to be born on her birthday. Well he did and guess what, three weeks later I again found out I was pregnant and my due date was her birthday. I knew I would have another c-section, so I knew this would work. I talked to my doctor and got it all planned. So I went along getting bigger and bigger again, but the pregnancy went great. This baby kicked me much more than Heather ever did, so something told me it was a boy. But, I thought how could both of my wishes come true? How cool would that be!

VIII

So the day finally came, and I once again had a beautiful baby and yes he was a boy. We named him "Benjamin (Boof) Harold Johnson," so he would have the same initials as his dad, but not be a junior. I believe everyone should have their own unique name. So he was born on July 11, 1986 (remember I told you to remember this date for you would see it again), so I now had my two children born on the same day 7-11, both weighing in at 7lbs. 11ozs., both 21 ¼ inches long and both perfect. Heather thought she got a brand new real doll baby for her birthday and immediately thought he was hers. She wanted to do everything for him; she was the perfect little mother. Billy had his son now and he was so delighted. My little girl came home from the hospital in a beautiful little dress and my son came home in camouflage (what can you say)? Once again we cried a lot. I had a little boy and he was also mine. I shared them with Billy, but they were mine. But we immediately realized that Boof had a health problem, so the doctors and testing soon began. None of the doctors could ever find anything wrong with him, but he was very sick. It would be 14 years later before we would find out what was medically wrong with him.

At this time it was 1987 and we had a very special day in our lives. It was on May 27, that my dad went to his first *Alcoholics Anonymous* (AA) meeting and believe it or not he never drank again. My family was back as a whole again. I think now of the courage and bravery it took for him to do this and what a wonderful person he turned out to be. It is amazing that someone can have that much strength to just stop an addiction that strong in one day, but he did. Maybe that's where I will end up getting some of mine from in the years to come.

IX

We all settled in with our family of four with Marie, Bonnie and I keeping all the kids all day, mostly at Marie's house. Marie had three; Peggy, Little John and Jenny. Bonnie had two and I had two, but we all actually had seven. We just all took care of all of them, for they were all like our own. With the help of my mom, Marie and Bonnie, I was taught how to be great mother and I followed right along. Marie was the boss during the day because she did have more practice. They always laughed at me because I had to go home at noon everyday for a nap, but I know they were just jealous. After nap time we went back to Marie's until Billy came home from work and we went out to eat or whatever we did. I never cooked in my life and as much as Marie was convinced that I was going to learn from her, it never happened so she finally got over it and quit. Her kids would go out with us and my kids would go eat real food at her house. Hey it worked out good for all. Those were the days! Life went on, I worked sometimes but I mostly had to stay home and take care of Boof due to his illness but we did ok thanks to help when we needed it. Our families were always there to help with whatever so life was good, but of course things would change again.

X

Now it was 1989, I turned 30, Heather turned seven and Boof turned three all in July. Billy and I separated in August and Hurricane Hugo came and wiped us out in September. Wow top that! Heather, Boof and I ended up on Wadmalaw Island in a trailer, because there was nowhere to live in Charleston due to all the damage. Billy was in N. Charleston, but believe me I never had to worry about anything. Billy was the greatest dad in the world (other than my own of course). I went to work at this time as much as I could to help with the bills, but I knew I never had to worry about anything as far as it came to raising my children. Billy had them on the weekends and I had them during the week, but he was also there a lot during the week also just because he wanted to be with his children. I respected him so much for this, for it made things so much easier for the kids. It all worked out great.

So Billy started dating someone who he would end up marrying and I also did the same. Little did I know the man I ended up marrying would end up being best friends with Billy, we were all just together all the time. It's like my kids ended up with two great dads (can't get any better than that). They had enough love around them for all the kids in the world. The years went by, but I did not get married for ten years. I went to college at the College of Charleston and Trident Technical College and ended up in nursing school which is what I always wanted to do.

Then Boof began to become sicker and things got very scary. He finally just had to be admitted to the hospital and went into major surgery to try to find out what was wrong and yes a miracle happened. He ended up with this wonderful doctor who just opened him up and found that he had been suffering from Hirschsprung's Disease, which meant that a portion of his colon was dead. The surgeon removed about two inches of his colon and we finally had a healthy perfect son. I was so excited that he was so healthy that I kept him out of school and just let him do all the things in life that he had never been able to do. It was amazing watching him just grow and finally enjoy every day. We had a blast just hanging out at the hunting club, or swimming, just anything we wanted to do. I home schooled him after that, but he never has to this day graduated from high school. We didn't care we were having the time with our son that we had never had.

Then I got married again to the same man I had been with for ten years on and off, graduated from nursing school, started working, and got divorced again all in about three years. I then came to the conclusion I suck at marriage, so if you have kept count that is three down and no more to come. If you are not any good at something you need to quit doing it, that's my new motto. I also know that I will never check the "other" box on the application for a marriage license. It has a first, second, third and other. I will not go there. They already knew me by name, so I think that would be too embarrassing to keep going back, it might begin to look like I'm the bad one and not the husbands (wouldn't want that).

XI

Then we all went through one of the worst times of our lives. Peggy, Marie and Johnny's oldest child was killed in a car accident out on John's Island. She was about 26 at the time, married and was about to graduate from MUSC with her Doctorate in Pharmacy. Until the day I die, I will never forget that phone call that morning and I will never forget my other daughter Peggy. I have never buried her although I know she is gone, but I know she is an angel in heaven looking down on all of us and taking care of us. I know she lets God help her family live their lives every day, but she will always be the worst loss in my life. I have lost all my grandparents, but you expect this. For they have lived long and happy lives and they are supposed to die, it is a part of life. We are all here with a plan from God and when it is our time to be angels we will go be them. That just doesn't make it any easier when it is someone young with their whole lives ahead of them. I have come to the conclusion that she will never leave us, we can always talk to her and I know she is there! God Bless my Peggy!

XII

Now the kids were about 14 and 18, Heather had graduated from High School and deciding about college and Boof was becoming a terror. When I say the word terror, I mean it very seriously. It only took a few years for me to come to know every judge, police officer, every jail in Charleston, Berkley and Dorchester Counties. It was all misdemeanor stuff like breaking restraining orders over this girl he fell head over heels in love with, but we finally just came to the conclusion that he liked it in jail so we let him stay there. The longest he was ever there was about 32 days, that was the one that finally taught him that he didn't want to go back and he didn't. But by this time I had had enough of his crappy attitude, lack of respect and plain not wanting to be a human being so I went the route of "tuff love." I got a Restraining Order against him to teach him that my days of his behavior were really over. I never saw him again for almost nine months and then saw him on Christmas Day, but only for about an hour. I was still not ready for his attitude which he had still not gotten right yet and I was sick of what he had put my entire family through, especially my mom and dad who would have done anything in this world for him and did many times. I have always loved my children no matter what, but I did learn that you sure do not have to like them all the time.

Heather got away from it all and went to *The California Culinary Academy* in San Francisco and became a Five Star French Chef. I have never and will never compare my children to each other, but this is when I decided that "Heather was my favorite child because she was my first, and Boof was my favorite child because he was my last!" I love them both no matter what they could ever do and yes Heather had her times, but boy did Boof make up for all the rest. It was kind of like God gave me the perfect child and then said "Oh no she needs more of a challenge than that for Heather was so easy," so I got my challenge! I can honestly sit back now and laugh a little about him and his challenges, and yes he has been forgiven by me for breaking my heart so many times, but he knows I will never forget them. That will teach him huh, yeah right!

Now both of my children are living on their own, I'm working as a nurse and loving life, *and then it happened…*

You hem me in – behind and before; you have laid your hand upon me. Such knowledge is too wonderful for me, too lofty for me to attain. Where can I go from your spirit? Where can I flee from your presence? If I go up to the heavens, you are there; if I make my bed in the depths, you are there. If I rise on the wings of the dawn, if I settle on the far side of the sea, even there your hand will guide me; your right hand will hold me fast.

*Psalm 139: 5-10 (King James Version)

CHAPTER TWO

My Illness

I

It was the night that changed my entire life, for the rest of my life. I never thought in a million years that someone could possibly hurt me so much that I would shut down completely; mind, body and soul. I know that this will be the hardest chapter for me to write. Please understand if I have to leave it every now and then, but I will be back to finish it. I believe this chapter of my book will lead you all to understand why I am taking on this task, because I know so many people have been and are now where I went to, so it has to be told.

It all began in April of 2006, when I met the man of my dreams, I will call him only X for this book. All he did was walk into my life and became my entire life from that point on. I gave him my heart, my soul, and all of my power. This was the man that I had waited my whole life for. Of all my marriages, it had never upset me when they ended. Of course I had to start a new life again, but it was no problem for me. I had thought that I had loved my husbands, but I had no clue what love was for a man until I met X. It seemed like he was the only person I could tell anything to, no matter how good or bad. He knew my entire life, from my childhood to all the problems that were in my life at that time. He also talked to me about his entire life, the good times and the worst of times. He had been through some very difficult times, but I understood him. We used to sit up all night and tell stories of our lives and make up the funniest stories. He had a sense of humor like me, so needless to say we laughed a lot. We loved the same music and danced in the strangest places, like on docks or anywhere we felt like it. I had great times with all his friends and we had great times with the friends we had together. He led me to believe that we would travel together and work together, so I thought this relationship was forever. We were going to live on the water which is my favorite place on earth and was also becoming his. To me it was like our souls were connected in some way, but who knew why.

In the first six months I tried to leave the relationship, because I thought it was getting more intense for me than for him. He always convinced me to stay and wait for things to happen, so I did. I did not realize that all he was doing was giving me "false hope." I did not know what this was until now, for I never would have done that to anyone. I had been married three times, but I had always been honest and true to my husbands. I have remained friends with them all to this day because we were all so good to each other. So as I learned more about him, I began to understand his problems with relationships, so all I could do was wait for him to believe in me.

I knew in my heart the way he felt for me, but he was just not in the right place to take it to the next level. I began to wonder at this time why he was trying so hard to make me stay. He knew I was hurting inside, but he always tried to make it right. So I kept believing in him and enjoying my time with him as he went on with his life and me with mine. After about a year, I really began to think that this was never going to work for me, the way things were going, but I never had the strength to leave him. My love for him was so strong that I would have done anything for him. I would have given anything to have spent the rest of my life with him. You see, I could see our future in my mind. My heart and soul were feeling emotions that I never had a clue about. I began to feel helplessness, jealousy, and need. It was so fabulous and I worked so hard for this, but things for him just kept getting farther and farther away from me and himself.

I was hurting my friends that had been in my life for so long. I would make plans with Sam or Linda and never show up, because he would call. I had turned into a different person because of him, a person that I never realized at the time I could ever become. It was like I knew they would understand, but would I have? The answer to this question is no and they had every right to be hurt by me. I will end up being very lucky in the end, but this will be later. X knew he was having problems with depression and was drinking more than he had ever had, and he began to worry about things more strongly. We talked about this a few times, but he wanted to just ignore it and hope it would go away. I tried to help him and tried to convince him to get help, but he thought he could handle them himself. He tried, but could not succeed.

Now it is about a year and a half into the relationship and I knew he was taking out his running shoes, this was how he always had left people in the past and he was getting ready to go again. I told myself at this time that this was just my imagination, because he could never leave me. Not me, this was too great of a relationship. For this was the most exciting, intense, and fun relationship that I have ever been in, so therefore; when he ended it on that hot night in just a matter of about five minutes there is no wonder the next years happened. This was June 2007.

II

I went into a complete shock and my entire mind and brain shut down. I do not remember getting home that night, but I know that I drove because my car was at home the next morning. I guess that is when the panic began, but I did not know at this point what was wrong. I began to become very dizzy all the time and very off balance (I thought that maybe I had a brain tumor or something) but had no idea what it was. The doctors started to diagnose me with vertigo and tried to medicate me, but it never seemed to help at all. At this point I had to completely quit working and at this point of writing I am still not working, it is now November 11, 2008.

This is when my fear started to set in, but of course I never realized that this was the beginning of the end. Therefore; the fear made the panic worse and then the depression started. The tears began about four weeks after this happened and they never stopped. After about two to three weeks, my mom came and put me in her truck and took me to the doctor in my pajamas. My mom and dad did not know what else to do. My doctor put me on my first antidepressant that made me sick as a dog, so that's when the medications started. We tried another and then another and this went on and on until I was so sick, losing weight which I didn't need to do. I am a very tiny person anyway with my average weight being about 107 lbs. I could not eat, sleep or function at all in any way. I had never had any kind of illness like this before in my life.

This is when Deb Dapore would become a very important person during my illness. She is my pharmacist that I have known for many years. I worked with her as her personal tech at Kerr Drugs years ago and we had a ball working together. She taught me so much about medications and boy was I sucking it all in. I was in nursing school at the time, so she became not only a great friend for life, but also a great teacher. Well I started calling her probably about five times a day asking her questions about so many meds that I was at that time trying. She would always encourage me to keep at it, that I would find the right drug eventually.

It became a morning ritual to call my sister Sharon and then Deb, and yes I did eventually wear them both out. Poor Deb she hung in there no matter what she was doing or how busy she was, she always talked to me. At this time she had opened her own pharmacy named "Plantation Pharmacy" on James Island and I was so happy for her. At this time I couldn't even really congratulate her, but now I sure can and I do. This pharmacy is such a "Deb" pharmacy with her old fashioned deli counter and her bottled cokes, how cool is that? Her staff is fabulous and if she was not there, they were always ready to help me also in anyway they could. The cutest little pharmacy in the world!

III

This is what sent to me a dear family that I have known for a very long time, the Poosers. Dr. Fred Pooser (Fred) is my first husband's cousin (remember I said you would hear about him later). Now he is a Psychologist and is in private practice. I did not know this until I had just taken care of his father in the hospital I was working at and the weird thing is, it was only about two months before this happened to me - I would realize later why. I had not seen them in years, but I now knew where to go, so I went. He diagnosed me with Catatonic Depression, Severe Panic Attacks and Anxiety. At first I never even cared that I was there and to this day I do not remember half the things he said to me, but I do remember the care and compassion he always gave me and the fact that he was always there for me whatever time of day or night. There were so many nights I called him in the middle of the night and he always talked to me and made me feel better. This I do remember. I continued to see him, but things for me just got worse. He was trying everything he could to help me, I guess my mind and brain just were not ready to begin healing. Now at this point of my life, I began to give up thinking I would not ever get better. I believed the only thing left for me was death at my own hand. The pain and fear had to go away somehow and I felt this was the only way to end it. *So I began to plan my death.*

This is when I fell off the cliff into the black hole. The worst parts of this hole were the darkness, it was so cold, that there was nobody else there and it was very deep. I knew at this time I would never have the strength to dig out of this hole, because I was so tired and so sick. Therefore; my plan began. I will not go into how I was going to do it, because being a nurse I knew how to die the first try and I don't want anyone else to know how to do this, so I will leave it there. So I set my plan in motion and began to play it out. I planned it at a time when it was not close to anyone's birthdays or any special occasions, because I did not want my children or my family's special days in the future to be destroyed by what I did. I thought it would just be another day and the notes that I was leaving them would allow them to go with their lives and understand that this was my choice and there was nothing that anyone could have ever done for me to make me not do it. This was the only way I felt they would forgive me and not hate me for leaving them. (I will stop writing now for a little while, you see this is very hard for me to bring back into my life, and it will only get harder). I will be back.

IV

I am back now, so here goes some more. The first thing I had to do was make sure that my children would be alright without me, so I rode to the ocean (Folly Beach ocean) and I said a prayer to God. I will quote you my prayer now. I do not have a date on it, but by the journals it had to be around the beginning of October of 2007. My prayer was, "Dear God, I know I have no choice now but to end my life to stop the pain. I pray to you to help me with my two children that you have blessed me with who have given me the greatest joys in my life. I am no longer able to care for them or be there for them so, I pray to you to please take them in your hands and take care of them for me. Please guide them through the rest of their lives by putting them in your hands, walking next to them when they are able to walk and carry them when they can not. I know in my heart that by giving them back to you, they will be safe and healthy for the rest of their lives on this earth and then they will spend their afterlife with you. For this God will bring me all the peace I will ever need after I go to hell for committing the ultimate sin of suicide. God I ask this of you and I thank you, for I have faith that my wishes for them will come true. Please understand that the pain is unbearable now for me to be here any longer, and I thank you for my beautiful life that you have given to us all and please forgive me for my sins."

So the first night I decided to end it all was in October, 2007, so I got my plan together and waited until my mom and dad went to sleep. My only problem now was that I did not want them to find me the next morning in my bed, so I decided to do it in my car. I got everything together and started to pick up the tools I needed, but instead I picked up the phone - I did not know why I did this at this time, but I will later. I called my mom, I remember screaming that I wanted to die and the time was going to be now. She came running into my apartment and she called Fred. He made her call 911 and they took me to St. Francis Hospital and he met me there. He got there before I did which was amazing. I think he must have flown.

I was put on suicide watch which is very degrading, but it had to be done. When I say degrading, I mean it. They watch you get undressed, check out all of your clothes and they put a guard at your door to watch you the entire time you are there. I had never been in jail before, but I felt like I was then. I don't remember much after the Ativan they gave me, but I agreed to go to Palmetto Lowcountry Behavioral Health for safety reasons. I signed the papers and was on my way. I went in on a voluntarily basis so I knew I could leave when I wanted to, but I knew I had to stay and try to get help. I went in with panic and depression and the first thing they did was lock the door behind me and the panic would immediately set in. I made it five days and that was enough for me. They were very nice and good to me, but I got no sleep, held on to walls I was so off-balance and it was very noisy. So my doctor let me go home and this was the beginning of the Palmetto days.

I hardly remember everyone at Palmetto, it's not that they weren't good to me; I just was not in the right frame of mind to remember it all. But there is one person that I will never forget and his name is William Mitchell. When I first walked onto Unit Two, I was crying so hard I could hardly walk or see anyone. But this great person came to me and handed me some verses from the Bible and told me to just start reading them out loud. I could hardly see the words because of the tears, but he just kept telling me to read and to read louder and louder. I did and then he gave me a big hug, I sat down next to him and he held my hand and I knew then I would be safe with this man. He was a person that wanted to help people and he truly tried in every way. There are very few times in one's life that you meet people that have found their purpose on earth and are actually living out their purpose, but as I continue to write you will find that I have been so lucky to find so many of them through this illness. Fred was first, then Deb, and then came William and there are many more to come.

At this time in my life is when I began to question what I had done so wrong in my life to deserve this from God. I will now quote a passage I had written in my journal one night; this was in (Jan. 2008) "I had always thought that I had been a good person, for my life's work was to help God's sick people. I had been a great mother, a good daughter and a good sister. I was always good to my friends. I knew that I had made mistakes in my life, but I never thought they were bad enough to not be forgiven for, but maybe they were. I began to believe that God did not want me on this earth anymore and that he wanted me to be with the devil, so this made me believe that committing the ultimate sin of taking my own life was his way of showing me that I was no good to him anymore. This was going to be my punishment for my sins that I had committed and would not ever be forgiven for." Then I started with but why me? I knew people that had done a lot worse things than I had ever imagined and they were not being punished, so why was I being punished in such a horrible way?"

I had been raised in the church as a child and was baptized at the age of nine, so I thought that God loved me. Then I thought that because I was not going to church every Sunday for the last years, that maybe I wasn't proving myself worthy of him. But in my mind I believed through these years that he knew where I was and what I was doing through my prayers, but I thought now that this was not good enough for him. I thought that I was supposed to be working or going to school to become a nurse and that was good enough. I had always been taught and always believed that you never questioned God for the decisions he made in your life, but now I was. I also believed that I had every right to question him because that is how your mind works down in the deep, cold, dark, lonely hole. But I kept wondering why nobody would come and get me out of this hole. I thought there were a lot of people in this world that loved me, but nobody came for me. Where were my children, my mother and father, my sister, my brother, my friends? I knew they were at my house, but why wouldn't they get me out of here?

I think I missed Heather the most, I couldn't figure out why she was not with me through these horrible times. I knew she was working, but where was she when she was off? I had always thought that we were so close as mother and daughter, but I was now even questioning that. She had just started dating someone new and it was like she wanted to spend all of her off time with him. I hated him for taking her from me, but it wasn't his fault, it was hers. She knew she had a very sick mother and did not even care. I don't want to hurt her feelings in anyway, but she sure hurt mine. I wanted her so bad that I would just holler out for her. I called her all the time and she would tell me she would be here as soon as she could, but she never came no matter how hard I cried she never came - I would later learn why. Benjamin was the one that surprised me by calling me all the time and coming to see me a lot more. He had no clue what to do with me either, but at least I felt like he tried. My how the tides had turned, it was like my children had become each other and switched places. It's like I was begging them to let me go, but nobody would when I had no purpose to be here. I was only awake about six hours a day at this time, so maybe this is why Heather never came over. What she didn't realize is that I was so scared to go to sleep was why I needed her so badly. It will take me a while from this time to understand why I was doing this, but at the time it was real and true. Life can be so sad and I had never been a sad person before. But, at this time little did I know, that the reasons would come to me. I would listen with all my heart and soul. They struck me like lightning, so strong and hard. This would end up being a good thing.

V

At this point the panic attacks were getting so bad, that I was having them in my sleep. I would wake up screaming because, I felt as though I was falling into some abyss and would have no control of my entire body. The only way to get them under control was to get back to the hospital and get intravenous Ativan and go back home. This was when most of the fear set in for me, because I began to think something really physically was wrong with me. With me being a nurse and had seen so many bad things go wrong that my mind just went off into all directions (brain tumors, spinal cord infections, Aids), everything that was life threatening entered my mind. At this point, I was on six milligrams (mg) of Ativan a day and still trying to find an antidepressant that would not make me so sick. But still found nothing to help me so I just kept at it.

I say I just kept at it, but things were getting so much worse for me, I wrote one night a very sad entry in my journal that I will share with you now. I wrote this on December 7, 2007, "A perfectly horrible day, I don't think they can get any worse. I cried all day and don't know why, dizzy all day. It must be the Ativan, but who knows or it could just be panic. Everything is just so horrible, oh just forget it. I don't want to even write about it. Yuk, Yuk, Yuk, nobody should have to ever live like this!"

Fred thought it was best at this time that I see a Neurologist too see if there was anything seriously wrong with me. I went to see a doctor that I had worked with as a nurse for many years and believed that he was the best there was in his field. He sent for an MRI which showed no abnormalities and then just said there was nothing else he could do for me. So the best doctor I thought I could see at this time ended up being the worst mistake that I think I had ever made. I found out quickly that he could care less about his patients or even if they died. Sorry if I tell it like it was, but I lost all respect for a doctor that I truly believed in. I hate to have to say this, but like I said this is a book of honesty and the whole truth. I may work with him again one day, but believe me he knows how I feel. I was still getting nowhere. But, I did get lucky enough to find another great doctor that sent me for the correct tests and gave the answers I needed.

It was around this time that Fred came up with a great idea to introduce me to another patient of his that was going through a lot of the same things I was going through. Her name is Hope Prioleau and we met one morning at Fred's office. I will not go into what her problems were, because that is nobody's business, but she was sick like I was. We met the next morning at James Island County Park to talk, but we were both too sick at this time to even begin to try to help each other. We came to find out that our families had been intertwined for the last 50 years. Her uncle and my father both worked for the same company for many years and were great friends for life. What a small world we live in was all I could think of at the time. Hope and I stayed in touch and talked when we could, but we would soon find that we had both found a great, very special friend for life.

VI

Now I decided to try my plan again, I really planned it this time because, I knew now I had to go. I could not go on another day like this, my life was over. So I set it all in motion again, but this time when I went to act out my plan, I picked up the phone again and called Sharon. I begged her to forgive me but I had to die now. I was crying so hard and just screaming for her to let me go. She came right over, got up in the bed with me, cried with me, and held on to me. But I knew where I was going again, so she went with me this time and stayed with me until I went back to Palmetto. I still could not understand why my plan was not working, why did I keep picking up that damn phone? I was furious with myself, because I knew this agony had to end, but why wasn't it? I was still in this black hole with no way of getting out, and nobody was coming to get me out. This time I stayed only three days, because I just could not sleep or eat there. I was now down to 95lbs. and things were just not helping. I was now starting Celexa (another antidepressant) and it was actually not making me as sick as the others did. I continued to take it and still am to this day.

At this point I had to start using a walker at times, because I was so off-balance. I felt so ashamed and sad because I thought people would laugh at me, but of course my family didn't and they were the only ones seeing me at this time. I think the worst part was that I was so scared to move. I was stiff as a board and could not move my head at all. It was like I was living like a blind person. I would spill things, drop things, and then I would have to wait for my mom to come clean up after me.

VII

At this time, Fred sent me to a Hypnotist named Karen Hoad so that I could start hypnosis. He felt that this really would help me and it did. It did not help in the beginning because I was so sick when I would go to see her, but she was so compassionate and wonderful to me. She would change her schedule and all to accommodate me in any way she could. I was so panicked and the Ativan was still making me so off-balance that it was hard to go anywhere, but my mom made me go and took me to every appointment for 16 weeks. I think my mom would have taken me anywhere at this point just to try to get me better. Even though I did not feel at the time that this was helping, boy would I believe in it later. It was one of the best things I have ever done for myself in my life. I got to keep a tape of every session and the more I listened to them, when I was at home and a little calmer the words really started to sink in. I would listen to the tapes and draw pictures of the places she took me and the things she had me do. She always took me to my favorite place the ocean, which would become my healing place. I also wrote this part which would stay with me forever: When it is sunny you will feel happiness, when it is cloudy you will feel peace and when it is stormy you will feel power. I would go back later and look at the pictures, but they still did not register in my mind yet. Her words were phenomenal and I will love her forever for all she did for me. I did not know this then - but once again I would later.

During these times I was still keeping in touch with some of my friends, Marie Mizzell, Linda Evans and Sam Shannon. I knew they were there for me, but I didn't think that anyone understood what this was like for me. They tried to cheer me up, but it never worked. Each played a different part in my life, some I talked to more than others. I thought of all of them all the time, but I was so jealous that they had lives and mine was gone. They were all still out there living their lives to the fullest, so I felt like I was kind of forgotten. I was scared to talk to Marie, my best friend of 28 years because she had gone through such a horrible loss in her life. I felt that I would upset her more talking to her about my loss. My loss was nothing compared to hers, but a loss of any kind can be like a death. She had lost her daughter, Peggy in a car accident about seven years before and I knew there could never be a loss as bad as that kind. Therefore; I never let her know how really sick I was until later, when things were becoming better for me.

Linda and Sam were also nurses and they had both moved out of state by now to work, and I missed them more than they will ever know. I wanted them to come home so bad, but they couldn't. I knew they had to go to other places, but since I wasn't thinking clearly I just felt as though they had left me. Sam and I had been such close friends for about ten years. We went to nursing school and all together, but I never really let her know how bad things were either. Linda and I had become great friends when we met working at MUSC and did almost everything together when I was not with X. When she left I had just begun to get really sick, but I told her I would be ok because I knew she had to go home and I did not want to make her feel sad for me. I feel she and Sam would have come home if they knew the real situation, but I did not want to interrupt their lives. I was also so ashamed of myself that I was so weak, and I didn't want anyone to know the truth. Believe me I would end up driving them all crazy soon.

The person that I talked to the most was Sharon, my goodness I know I drove her crazy. I would call her at least ten times a day, but she understood what this was like to a point. She had suffered some depression after my niece was born, so she could relate in some ways. Bless her heart she always had kind words to say to me and never made me feel like I was bothering her. when I knew I was but I didn't care at the time, all I knew was that I needed her and she was there.

It was getting close to Christmas now and of course I was not able to do anything. I wrote in my journal one night on December 24, 2007 and I will quote it to you now, "It's Christmas Eve and has been a very sad day for me, last year was such a happy time and this year is so bad. Everyone is so busy and nobody has time for me, but that's ok, I will just have to be ok with it all and try to go on. I just miss everyone so much and the loneliness is killing me. I hate myself for being so weak!"

VIII

The next part of my story is a part that I never want my family to know, but of course they will now. When I started this book, I promised myself I would tell all and I would be honest to the world. I plan on talking to my parents about this situation before they read it, so they will not be hurt in any way. I plan to take them to my doctor's office and tell them there, because I think having my doctor there will help them to understand where my mind was at this time. That is the least I can do for them, after all they have done for me. My mom and dad had started going to church at this time. I think they were trying anything to get me better, because they just had no clue what to do for me anymore. This is the main reason for this book to let you all know what I now know I needed, so you will be able to help loved ones or friends or anyone else, if you are ever faced with this kind of situation.

I was now trying to get off of so much of the Ativan, because the doctor at Palmetto thought maybe that was causing the unsteadiness and imbalance. I was in such bad withdrawals and so very sick, I had missed all of the holidays with my family and I was missing everything in life. I could not go on like this for another day. So my parents went to church, which I knew they were going that Sunday morning in February and this was going to be the time. I was in my apartment which is connected to their house and I walked up to there house looking for someone, anyone, but there was nobody there. I knew I was in serious trouble at this time, but I could not find anybody. *As I was coming back down the hall is when I saw it!* My dad's gun was sitting right there in his bedroom by his bed. I knew I finally had a way out, so I got the gun and also got lucky enough to find bullets right

31

there on the night stand. I felt so relieved at this moment, I did not know what to do with myself, all I knew was now it was going to be over, and I think I may even have smiled. So I got the gun and bullets and took it to my apartment. This is the shocker, I could not figure out how to load it and use it. Now I am a person that has been around guns all my life, two ex-husbands were hunters along with my son, so I had shot every kind of gun there was. I used to even load my own bullets, but now I could not figure out how to load a 22 shotgun. This was ridiculous! I kept trying for as long as I could before my mom and dad came home, but I could not figure it out. I was panicked so badly at this point, I had no idea what to do next.

I remember telling God that if he really wanted me to go to the devil, then let me load this gun or if he wanted me to stay on this earth and continue to do his work then take the wisdom from me to load the gun. Well he took the wisdom from me and this became a huge turning point in my life. I didn't really understand why God would leave me here to stay in this hole, but I would understand this later also. My parents got home and I had to put the gun back quickly, and told them I had to go back to the hospital. I did not tell them what I had done.

I went back to Palmetto for the last time and vowed I would never go back there, because this place just was not helping me. The hardest part of writing this part of my plan is that I never want my parents to feel guilty about leaving a gun in their house in full view with a suicidal daughter that could get her hands on it at anytime. But they have nothing to ever feel guilty about because, I had made many promises to them that I would never actually do anything to hurt myself. They trusted my promises, but they did not understand that I would have promised anybody anything at this time, to just get my plan over with so I would never have to live another day like I was. This would have never been their fault in any way, it's just how the illness works because the loneliness is just too much to handle. I pray they will understand this and not hate me for it, for this would also be too much to handle. I know that my parents are very strong, but I also ask myself "How strong are parents supposed to be in a situation like this"?

IX

At this time it was becoming inevitable that the doctor at Palmetto was not helping me, so Fred, Karen and I started looking for a new doctor. To find a Psychiatrist in Charleston is nearly impossible, for they all had waiting lists and nobody could take me on. I felt so hopeless and lonely I just didn't know what to do. This was around (March 2008) that I decided to ride to the beach for the first time by myself. I just felt like if I was near the ocean I could find some answers as to what to do. Therefore, I drove there and just sat in my car at the washout. I was crying so hard that I had no clue how I was going to get home, but I didn't even care. I started crying out for God to please come to me and help me and before I realized it I was actually screaming for him. *It was then that my entire life would change.*

I know this is going to be hard to believe but all of a sudden I felt this hand on my shoulder. I knew it was a hand, but I was by myself in the car and didn't see anyone, I could not figure out who it was. Then if came to me, God was there with me and he was letting me know it. I just started talking to him and trying to thank him as much as I could for being with me and that he was finally there. I began to feel like the luckiest person on the face of the earth, for this is when I found faith and hope. It was this same day that Fred called me and told me that he had a dear friend named Dr. Joseph Zealberg (Dr. Z) and he agreed to take me as a patient, "Could this really be happening to me"? I only hoped at this time that I would still be able to see Fred also. I didn't know what I would do without him, he had saved my life so many times that I could never count them. There was never a time when I could not reach him and he would always make me feel better no matter what he had to do. There were many times he would even meet with me on Saturday or Sunday, which was his time to rest. But he was more concerned about me and my well-being. I will never forget one time when I was at Palmetto, heard the doors open and there he was. Wow, that was really beyond the call of duty, but he was there. I knew he would put me in good hands and this he did.

Dr. Z. was on James Island also, so that made him closer to home and easier to get to him. My first appointment was for one and a half hours. I had to start all over again and go through all of this again which was very hard but at the end of the session he said to me, "Cindy, it's going to be ok now, we are going to get through this and you will get better." I think these were the best words I had ever heard in my life. I was still crying all the time, but something was now happening to my tears. When I left Dr Z's office I cried all the way home but these tears felt different, they kind of had a feeling of hope in them.

X

I had written in my journal at one point something that William told me. He told me that we were all born with a tool box inside of us and that this tool box was given to us from God and it was to be used for healing in times of trouble. It goes like this: In this tool box we have a hammer for faith, a screw driver for strength, and a pair of pliers for courage, and a box of nails and screws. All the tools were given to us; we just had to learn to use them. We could hammer another nail when we needed more faith, we could screw in another screw when we needed more strength, and we could use our pliers when we needed more courage. At the time I was told this, I just shrugged it off like yea right, like I was given this. I think God forgot to put mine inside of me. Little did I know at the time how important these words would become in my life? I guess that is what it was - I will know for sure later.

The first thing Dr. Z. started working on was getting me off the Ativan and on the correct meds that would help me. He put me on Klonopin, Neurontin, and left me on the Celexa, but he also left me on the Ativan for two weeks for the other meds to get into my system. Then I started cutting back on the Ativan and believe it or not I had no withdrawal symptoms at all. He also knew that the imbalance and unsteadiness was from panic, not the meds. When the meds started working well, I started eating better, crying less, and walking a lot less with the walker. Something was beginning to happen to me, I did not know what it was yet - but I would later. After a few meetings with Dr. Z., I knew that I had met yet another person that was doing what they were born to do. It was like he and Fred were born from the same mold. For Dr. Z. also had all the compassion and caring for his patients as Fred did. He told me that he would always be available for me which was what I never had with my doctor at Palmetto. This made me feel calmer and safe knowing that he thought of me as a person and not just another number that he had to take care of.

I began to enjoy my visits with Dr. Z. and looked forward to seeing him the next time. At this time, I believe that I could see a little bit of light at the end of the hole. I can almost be sure it was light, because I could feel hope. Little did I know how hard it would become to start digging out of that black hole, but I was beginning to figure out how I could try to find a way. All I knew at this time was that I was going to do it some way or the other and not stop until I did, *so I started my journey of release…*

Notes

Notes

Notes

Notes

Notes

Notes

Notes

Notes

Notes

Notes

Then shall ye call upon me, and ye shall go and pray unto me, and I will hearken unto you. And ye shall seek me and find me, when ye shall search for me with all your heart. And I will be found of you saith the LORD: and I will turn away your captivity, and I will gather you from all the nations, and from all the places whither I have driven you, saith the LORD: and I will bring you again into the place whence I caused you to be carried away captive.

*Jeremiah 29: 12-14 (King James Version)

CHAPTER THREE

Finding Faith, Strength, and Courage
(Climbing Out)

I

Now I am at the bottom of this very deep hole seeing a little bit of light, but I can not figure out how I am going to get out. It has become obvious to me that nobody is coming for me, but I know now that there is a presence with me because I can feel someone. I know that God was with me at the ocean and I am now thinking that it is him with me now. I do still doubt why he has not gotten me out yet, but I feel that I am getting some answers to my prayers. I am so sick now, so weak, so cold and so lonely that I have no idea how I will ever get the strength to get out of here, but I do know that I must start trying or I will die here and I am not ready to die.

I want to see my children get married and have children and this is all I am thinking about now. I miss helping people at work and I am beginning to feel that I need to be back there doing what I am meant to be doing. I don't really know how to describe it, but I am feeling like my brain and my mind is beginning to change in some way, but I do not understand yet what is happening to me. I spend my days sleeping a lot and I am still so unsteady on my feet. I can not watch television or listen to music because of the dizziness, but all I know is that I have to do something and do it fast.

So I begin to think about my tool box that I have built inside of me and I start thinking that if I could only learn how to use it maybe it would help me, so I start thinking. Little did I know that my journey of release would take a very long time and would be the hardest thing I would ever take on and accomplish, *so I began…*

II

I am still seeing Dr. Z. about every week now and beginning to feel like the new meds were working better at this time. I was so anxious for things to change in my life, but the feelings of wanting to die just would not go away. When I would look up and see how far I had to go to get out of the hole I was in, it seemed so impossible. I became very frustrated, but I think this would end up being a good thing because I began to get mad. I was mad at myself for letting this happen to me when I did nothing wrong. But then again I did do something wrong, I gave away my power and now I must get it back. So I began to think about how I would do this and once again I looked to God.

I began to pray a lot and just beg him to show me how to use my tools he gave me. This is when I think I realized that if he gave me these tools, then that was his way of helping me get out. I then began to picture my hammer, screw driver and pliers in my mind and began to think about what they would give me. Faith, Strength, and Courage were the key words here and I knew I had better start understanding them soon, for I wanted to go home so bad it hurt. I wrote a poem one night, it was around (March 2008) and I will write it for you now. This poem was written for my friend Linda, but boy would it become me also.

Home
Love is a choice, one worth making,
no matter how hard, the road is worth taking.
The steps will be short and the road will be long,
but the journey will lead us to a place called home.

The beauty inside us will show the way,
the lights above us will show it's ok,
our souls will guide us all the long way,
for the journey has just begun.

If the journey becomes too long or gets too hard,
just remember one thing and remember it hard,
the past was a lesson, only to be learned,
not a way of life to only yearn.
So take these lessons on your journey so hard,
follow the moon and follow the stars,
for they will shine, but only when you find home!

As I wrote this poem for Linda, it was a good time before I realized that it would become mine also. So now I share it with her and we will both find home. I knew she would never mind sharing this poem with me because we are partners in everything we do in life. If only she knew how much she was missed by me.

III

The first thing I had to do was to find my faith and start believing in myself again and make myself start the process of coming out. Dr. Z. believes in me so much and gives me such hope, that I am truly beginning to believe that I can do this. This is what would lead me to think about all the times that I tried to end my life and never went through with it. I asked myself a million times why my plan never worked and there had to be a reason. I tried so hard to make my plan work, but there was like this power that would come over me and stop me. I began to ask myself "Is it truly God that wants me here? Maybe there is a reason he wants me here on this earth longer. Could I actually be good enough for him to come to me and help me?"

At this time I was still using a walker, was so panicked I was afraid to even go to sleep or walk out of my own house. But my mind and my brain were beginning to think in a clearer way. Believe me, I was still fuzzy most of the time, but something was happening to me. This is when I got my hammer out of my tool box, got my nails and started to really get mad. I took that hammer and I began to hammer, hammer, and hammer hollering for God to come to me and let me know what to do. Then I began to climb, but I was so tired and sick I could not get anywhere. This would only make me madder so I started hammering some more. I began to get off the ground, but I would fall back down to the bottom again and again. It was like I would get three steps up and fall two steps back, then I would have to rest some more. When I rested I would look up to that little bit of light way up there in the sky (that was one deep hole) and I would talk to God. I would just say anything and everything on my mind, but now I was beginning to feel like he was listening because I was learning what my tools were for and how to use them. He gave them to me, but I had to use them. I guess that is what the healing process is about - you have to do the work.

IV

I feel like my hammer is doing something now, so I decided to learn how to use my screw driver and try to find some strength. I relate strength to fear, because I am so scared of everything at this time. Maybe if I could become strong again, I could let go of the fear. I wrote in my journal one night about fear, I will quote it now (no date again, must be around January 2008). "What really is fear? It is being scared to do something outside of your box. Then why am I so scared to do things I have done all of my life? I am not even able go riding in my car, eat at my mom's house, and I will never sleep on my right side again, for that's when the panic attacks would happen in my sleep all because I am scared of panic attacks. I must overcome my fear and get on out of this hole and get on with my life. How? *By doing it*!

I am about out of nails now so I must start screwing in screws. Believe it or not the screws seemed to go in easier. So I started screwing them in and I am finding that I am getting a little farther up the hole, not much but some. Rest is all I want to do, but I am beginning to realize that this will get me nowhere, so I just keep on going up some more and falling back down, going up some more and falling back down, but you know what I am getting farther each time. I am realizing that I have to start eating better for energy, so I do. I have no muscle mass at this time from doing nothing for so long, so I have to find some strength somewhere, and guess what God will be the answer again. I prayed for faith and I received it so now I am praying for strength. I am telling God that if I ever get out of this hole, I can go back to taking care of his sick people and do his work for him for the rest of my life on earth. I sometimes felt like I was maybe trying to make a deal with him, but what else could I do? I did not know what else to do, but I would find out later that making deals with God was not the answer, just believing would be. This lead me to believe that my faith was growing stronger, so I knew my strength would too.

I kept screwing in my screws, climbing and climbing, falling and falling, then I would hammer some more nails, start climbing and climbing, falling and falling, but getting farther every time. Now something was really happening, the light was getting brighter and brighter. It was no longer dark in the hole, yes it was still cold and lonely but I did not feel alone as much. This is when I knew God was really with me and guiding me to do the work I had to do. This is when something really incredible happened.

51

When I would think I was going to run out of nails or screws, I never did. I always had as many as I needed, but where were they coming from? The only person with me was God, so I guess he was the one filling my box up when it started to get low.

V

This is when my heart and soul began to open up again and I felt like I could feel things again. The pain was not as strong as it was and I did not feel as lonely anymore. I was beginning to miss Sharon a lot, but she was taking care of her mother-in-law at this time who was very sick. I would still call her all the time and she always took the time for me. I missed everybody in my life, but it was different now. Believe it or not I was getting out of the house some by myself. I would ride to the beach and look at the ocean all the time. I always knew the ocean was a place sent to us for healing, so there I went. The greatest thing was I was by myself! I cried all the time I was at the beach, but the tears are really different now. It was like I was entering a new world, but I did not know where I was going to. God was sending me there and I was beginning to realize that everything that was happening was because he was guiding me there.

I kept on hammering and screwing my nails and screws and I was getting farther out of that hole. God was giving me more strength now and I was more powerful. I remember thinking "I will do this and I will be alive again, I will do it." My hypnosis had been finished for a long time now, but now is when it would start helping me a lot. In my mind I could take myself to all the places Karen had taken me and I would become calmer and find more of what I needed inside of me. One thing she put in my subconscious mind was that "The wind would bring change." Now it was around (May 2008) and it was windy a lot. I remember I would sit and just watch the wind and pray for change.

At one time Karen took me to a beach where I was by myself and there were the numbers 1-5 in the sand. As I would start to erase the numbers with my foot the ocean would start coming closer and closer to the numbers. As I erased #5, I had to do it alone, then came #4 and the ocean came up a little bit further and touched the number, but I still had to do it alone. As I got to #3, the ocean came up more and helped me erase the number, then came #2 and the ocean came and helped me more and then the ocean erased #1 by itself. This was to make me believe that it would get easier as I went along and did the hard work that was facing me. For if I only believed I could do it, it would happen. I could feel it coming, but there was one more thing I needed at this time, this would be courage.

VI

When I think of courage the first thing I had to do was look up the meaning of the word, I had to know that I was going in the right direction. The meaning of the word courage is: the quality of being brave; valor. The word valor means: marked courage of bravery.

Now I had to connect my faith and my strength to the act of bravery to find the courage I needed to continue this climb. It also brings to me the act of fear which is in my mind the reason I am not out of this hole yet, but I must now learn how to let courage take me to the end. I am finding that the hammering of the nails was very hard, the screwing in the screws was easier, so using my pliers must be the answer. Now I prayed to God to let the ocean come up further and help me more, because I knew that courage would set me free. *So I began...*

I looked inside myself to my tool box again and I got my pliers out, but I was not sure at this point what to do with them. Then once again God showed me the way and I started to remove the nails and screws that I had worked so hard to put in, and I continued to climb. I am still so tired, scared, lonely and cold, but now I have light. I can see the top of the hole more and more as I get closer and closer, but why do I still keeping going back down? I ask myself, am I not working hard enough? I will quote another passage from my journal from (June, 2008) "Why do I sit and be so scared when all my life I haven't been? Do I do it to myself when all I have to do is let go? The hopes and dreams I have for my life are so incredible, but I fall back down and wait for another time, so life goes on and I still wait to take the easy road. But not any longer, my mind is made up to start to live for me. To let it go for me will be hard, for it is all I have ever known, but I will use my strength and all the will and pull it out somehow. No longer the hole! I will cover it up with faith, strength, courage, hope and trust and this I will do because fear is no longer sitting here to keep me from my life!" (Please remember that when I wrote these passages in my journal I was medicated and not thinking clearly, but this is how I want you to see the truth of how a person can think when they are this ill. Please try to read the meaning of what I am trying to say, even though at this time I do not even know).

At this point in my life it's around July 2008, all of our birthdays are coming up and I am still not able to do much. Dr. Z. wants me to try to get out of the house more, so this is what I am trying to do. I am ok in the car by myself, but getting out of it is a whole different story. He is trying to teach me to re-train my brain by going into public places as I have always done, so that my brain will re-connect that it is ok for me to be there. My first outing was to Marie's house where I have been safe for 28 years of my life. I got out of the car and went inside. I had mentioned before that I did not want to bring back bad memories for her with my sadness, but she then told me that it was ok, she needed to talk about Peggy so that she would never be forgotten. I started wondering how she got through her ordeal and she shared a lot good things with me.

I was shaking all over but I did go inside of her house and about five minutes later I left. I was so proud of myself I didn't know what to do. I cried and cried the whole way home, good tears. Yeah! I had gotten out of that car. I started talking to Marie a lot more now and feeling more comfortable with her situation and she became a huge help to me, it showed me that if she could get through what she had to go through, then I would be able to too. Was I finding courage at this time, well only time would tell? I then told myself that the next day I was going to go into a public place by myself, so I picked Walmart and started preparing for this event. The next day came and off I went. I got there and just sat in my car and built up my courage for about ten minutes, smoked two cigarettes and got out of the car. I was shaking so bad I could hardly walk, what people do not understand is that the shaking and the fear is uncontrollable. It is your brain working not correctly and I mean not correctly! I walked up to the door of Walmart opened it and went inside. Well, I do not even know how to put into words what happened to me, all I know is I got the hell out of there and I got out fast. I then sat in my car for about 15 minutes trying to calm myself down, remembering the places Karen had taken me to in hypnosis and I was finally able to drive home. (Remember I said before that I didn't realize how important hypnosis would end up being for me, well now I am realizing it). But I could tell you at that time Walmart would never be a part of my life again - but it did later.

This is when I was beginning to learn the meaning of the phrase "unshakable faith." I now know God is with me every second of every day and keeping me safe now. I also was beginning to realize that courage was going to be the hardest thing I would ever have to learn again. To have courage you have to let the fear go, well good luck to me, it seemed an impossible task.

VII

Well the only thing I knew to do then was continue with my pliers and keep taking the nails and screws out. Then I would hammer the nails back in and screw the screws back in, but the most important thing was that I continued to climb and climb. I think I was over half way up the hole now, but of course I still kept falling back in. So I kept at it and kept getting farther and farther up. Wow the pliers were really getting easier and easier to use, maybe the ocean was coming up and doing most of the work for me now. I was beginning to feel hope that I was going to get this job done, and that felt good.

This is when something really incredible happened to me, *I realized that I no longer wanted to die, now I wanted to live*! I wanted to live my life and do all the tasks that God would give to me and I wanted to do them well. I have always known that my purpose on this earth was to help others and I was beginning to want to do this again. It was now not all about me, but about what I could do for God and his people on earth. I will always remember this turning point, because it would be the most important time in my life ever. I remember telling Dr. Z. that I was getting happier, smiling, and laughing some now. He smiled at me and looked at me like he was so proud of me for the work I was doing. He knew now that I was really going to do this and once again he told me so. The encouragement he gave me at all times will always be priceless to me. There are times in life when you go to a doctor and things just don't feel right, like there is a lack of trust or feeling like they really do not care about your well-being. Well, I think I have now put together "The Dream Team", and OJ thought he had it, well he had no clue. I was beginning to feel like the luckiest person in the world. It was almost like the elation I felt when I had my children, yeah! *I was going to live and I was going to make it!*

Guess what I did now? I continued to hammer nails, screw screws and work those pliers like a wild woman. I had found courage and once again it came from God. Now I had faith, strength, and courage, wow! Things were getting easier and easier and I was getting out of that hole. I felt warmer, less lonely and most of all less fearful. Yes, the panic was still there. The panic attacks were not occurring as much at this time. Don't get me wrong, this does not mean that I was not scared every second of every day that they would come back, but for some reason it was ok. I think I had learned that I was not going to die from them, even though you feel like you are. My anger was getting stronger and stronger which gave me the energy to keep going, and I kept going. I think a miracle was in the process of being made, but who knew how much of one - only time would tell.

VIII

At this time I was only writing in my journals every now and then, for I had much more important things to do. I had to get well and that is all that was on my mind. I was getting closer and closer to the top of that hole and I began to really believe I was going to get there. Now I started thinking what was I going to do when I got out? Was my life going to be the same as it was before? Would all this hard work be over? Could I just rest for a while and not be scared? My mind just started racing with questions, so I took them to Dr. Z. He explained to me that the healing process would be a long one, but that it would get easier as time went on. He also explained the process of patience and that I would have to have a lot of it. Well, I have never had any of that in my life. Patience was not even a word in my dictionary, so I contemplated this and decided it was something I could learn, look at all the other things I had learned in the last year. This should be a breeze, little did I know. This word is still not in my dictionary and this is a long time later (January 2009).

Ok now my anger is turning to getting pissed off and I am very tired of this. I am sick of hammering, screwing and using pliers. I want out and I want out now! So once again I turned to God, and started begging him to come to me again, I promised everything again and again and again. I knew he was there, but I wanted him to push me over the top of this hole and I wanted it now. Once again my answer was, yes Cindy I am here, but if you do not do the work you will never heal properly and I do not want you to ever have to go through this again. I was thankful for these words, because I knew one thing and one thing for sure, *I did not ever want to go through this again and I knew I could never live through this again*!

Then there was another sad time in our lives, Sharon's mother in law was becoming very sick now and was not expected to live much longer. Sharon had become very close to her and her son Barry had taken great care of her for the last two years that she had been so sick. Her son Barry Waldrop would now become a very important part of my life at this time. I had worked with Barry years ago when he and Sharon opened the first "*Stono Café*" on James Island and I used to work with them. We had a great time working together, but were never really what you would call great friends.

Well it is amazing how people are put back in your life in such a different way when you need them the most. So God sent me Barry! He knew he could give me more courage and yes he did. It had been about 20 years since I had seen Barry and I just happened to talk to him one night on the phone when Sharon was at his house. We talked about so many things, and for some reason Barry understood what I needed. I thought maybe he was a mind reader, but he was a gift. We met at the James Island County Park the next morning and just sat and talked. He was also going through a hard time with his mother's condition so we were like two lost souls come together to help each other. We talked for about an hour, this was the longest I had been anywhere in over a year, but I felt comfort with him. We cried, we laughed, and then he taught me his motto in life which is "Just keep on walking harder and faster girl, cause we ain't got no time for this shit today!" Well I repeated these words to myself about a thousand times a day, every time I would get upset and they really did work.

I began to talk to Barry a lot at this time and believe it or not I even went to his house one day. This is a day that I will never forget because I got to see Nana, his mother, but I did not know that I would never have the chance to see her again. As sick as she was she told me to come and sit by her and she took my hands in her and she told me "Don't worry honey, for this too shall pass." What an incredible woman she was, she was not worried about herself, she was worried about me. This time with her taught me the meaning of the word strength and that I could become well. She was so strong up until the very end of her life. I talk to her a lot now and imagine her resting on a cloud with her husband and I tell her thank you for her wonderful words, because they did change my life. To have so much courage while being so sick seemed to come easy for her. I still hear her telling me these words all the time as I talk to her and she never lets me forget them. I for sure never will, for this will be a huge turning point in my life.

IX

One of the biggest things I learned in hypnosis is how to turn negative things into positive ones, well I was still in the process of learning how to do this and the next few months would teach me that I really could do this and what a relief I would feel. Nana passed away in May of 2008 and Sharon and Barry were going through a terrible loss. I started going to Barry's a lot with Sharon and sitting outside on the Lanai and it sort of became like going to therapy sessions.

The incredible part of it was that I felt like I was beginning to help them and being a support system for them. I would leave there feeling like I was worthy or something and my need for helping others was coming back to me and in a very strong way. After a few weeks we began to not mourn so much over Nana's death, but to celebrate her life while she was here with them.

I wrote a poem for Barry and I will tell it for you now.

A PIECE OF HEAVEN

This piece of Heaven is a special place of
friendship, family, and fun.
I guess the fun is the best part
cause you never know when it will come.
you can even get wobbly, or even fall on your face,
for nobody really cares:
we may talk about you late, but oh what the hell!
we all need a good laugh now and then
and you can always find it there.

It's also a place of therapy and healing
twenty four hours a day,
You can cry if you want to, there is always a hug there.
The friendship and the love is felt so very strong,
for Otis will even love you if nobody else is home.
This place even has a pool, a beautiful, warm one at that
and lordy you can do anything there
believe me I know that!
How could this place get any better?
well now I will tell:

Nana, Barry, Sharon and Otis make up this beautiful place,
but I am very lucky too, for I have been
invited to share it with them too.
I pray every night that I will get to go back,
for a place of such peace is so very hard to find,

now I know God loves us all
in spirit and in our time.

Yes, this place has a name, for this I will tell you soon,
"The word means beauty, flowers, love and health,
how perfect a name for a perfect place
"The Lanai"

(July 2008)

Just by being there with them and having so much support from God, Heather, Boof, Mom, Dad, Barry and all of my friends, I finally got to the top of the black hole and believe it or not *I climbed out of it*! *I climbed out of it*! *I climbed out of it*!

I can try to explain the moment when I realized I was out, but I can not put it with a certain situation or time. It must have been around (July 2008), but the feeling of freedom was very real. All I knew at this time was that God had given me the tools, guided me all the way, gave me the support of my family and friends, and he stayed with me the entire time.   Everywhere he sent me I now realized was for a reason.

He sent me to Fred, then to Karen, then to Dr. Z. and this whole time he had a plan for me. He made me do the work, but he watched over me and kept me safe. He listened to me beg and plead, but he understood. He let me scream and have doubt, but he showed me the truth. He gave me faith, strength and courage, and then he led me to the top. I have always heard the saying that "God will never give you more than you can handle," well the next thing I learned was how he taught me the things I needed to learn, and then when I learned them well enough for this to never happen to me again, *he gave me freedom*.

Please understand that this did not bring complete wellness, for I had a long way to go, but I covered that hole up with dirt so nobody else could ever fall in it and I celebrated with tears and joy. Other people could probably tell you when this happened just by being with me better than I can, especially Sharon. All I can say is "poor Sharon," the things she went through with me, the twenty phone calls a day, the tears, the hospital visits when she sat with me the whole time. My sister had become the sister I had wanted all my life and now I finally had her. If it takes the rest of my life, I could never thank her enough for being there and believe me I will never let her go again. Please believe me when I say it was not just her, it was my mom and dad, my children and everyone, I had worn them all out by now and they had no clue as to how much longer I would be continuing this. I felt sorrier for my family than I did for me.

So now I am out of the hole, but I have no idea what to do next to continue my healing process, but it would not take me long to see that I had lost all of my coping skills. So guess what now I have to learn them again, *so here goes...*

CHAPTER FOUR

Coping
(Learning Again)

I

When I said it would not take me long to find out that I had to learn coping skills again, well it didn't. I guess I thought that when I got out of the black hole my life would be there waiting for me just the way it was before I fell in it, but it wasn't. I could not find my life anywhere and I looked everywhere. I had nothing left, it was like all the strength and courage I had found in the hole was gone.

Coping means to be able to successfully deal with a difficult problem or situation. I had always been able to do that before, so I thought this would be no problem I would just do what I had always done before. That is where the problem came in, I had lost my skills and had no idea how to get them back. I felt guilty about everything, I had fears of everything and my feelings were all over the place. I still felt like I was the only person on the earth and I didn't know how to find anybody. My mom and dad were right here, but I couldn't see them. The only thing I did know was that God was with me and he wanted me here, so I had better get on with it.

I was seeing Dr. Z. once a month now because I did not have the money to see him more and my parents were paying all of my bills. I had not paid anything for about six months now and the guilt was eating me up. I knew that they did not mind, but they are not rich and could not afford this, but believe me they would have done anything to make sure we all had everything we needed. I remember going to Dr. Z's office one day and he came out and said "Come on back Cindy, how are you doing today?" My response was "I am so frustrated I can't stand it." He replied with, "Well we do frustration here too!" That was a good thing because I really was frustrated. I had no job, no life, no patience and no hope for any of these things in the near future. Of course he made me feel all better by telling me to slow down, it would all work out and that all of these things that I was feeling were completely normal. I liked hearing the words "completely normal," they made me feel normal (whatever normal was, I didn't remember).

II

It did not take me long to realize that the guilt I was carrying around with me was one of the biggest reasons that I could not cope. During my illness my parents, my children, and my entire family had to deal with all of my life. They had to see me in a situation that was truly horrifying. I could never imagine one of my children every lying in a bed in front of me and asking me to just let them die. Well this is what I had done to my parents. How could I ever put them through something like this? If I would have known at the time what I was doing, believe me it would never have happened, but now I had to deal with it. I had also used up almost all of their retirement money and I had no idea how I was ever going to repay them. I also felt like I was letting my patients down because I was no longer there to take care of them. I could not cook for myself, go buy my own groceries, or even take care of myself in so many ways. About all I could do for myself was take a shower, and keep my apartment kind of clean.

My mom and dad were doing everything for me and they were getting exhausted. I can not count all the trips to the hospital they had taken me to, and they always stayed with me and made sure I was ok. They had to admit me to Palmetto three times, to Roper twice and many emergency room visits that took hours each time. I wanted to stay at the hospital many times just so they could go home and get a few days rest. But they never stayed home, even if I was admitted they always came to see me, or Heather or Sharon would come and see me and stay with me. The guilt was getting to the point where suicide was beginning to look like the only answer out again, and this I would never do to my family after all they had done for me, so I had to find a way to cope with it. *I found it through forgiveness.*

III

I had to forgive myself for getting sick, something that I had no control over. I had to make myself realize that this was not something that I had asked for, it just happened. I then asked God for more advice and to teach me how to do this. I had forgiven my son for all that he had put me through; I had forgiven my daughter for not understanding what to do with me when I was so sick, and I had even forgiven X. But why was I having such a hard time forgiving myself? Maybe it was because this was a new concept for me, I had never had to forgive myself before which was a good thing. It made me feel like I had been a good person during my lifetime and had lived my life in a good way. I believe now that the problem was that I just had so much guilt inside of me I didn't know where to begin. All I knew at this time was that I was going to have to be patient (that damn word again that I still don't get) with myself and just pray for more strength and courage to help me. I didn't know how much strength and courage each person on this earth was allowed, but I sure knew that I had probably used up all of mine. I was so tired and sick I didn't think I could take on another challenge. But I had to try so I began, so I began the next journey.

The first thing that I had to do was convince myself that this was what my parents and family wanted to do for me. They wanted to help me get well and that is what they wanted in their hearts. I knew that I would do anything for any of them no matter what, but that was not what was important. I had to let that go, for that was a given and they all knew I would be there for them. I just had to believe in my heart that they all loved me so much they would do anything. This is what finally brought me peace and let the process begin. I started turning the negatives into positives again (hypnosis again came into play a lot here) and remembering the things that would be possible. When I got my disability I would be able to pay my parents a good bit of money back, this helped a lot. Then I started thinking that if I could get out of this house more, I could do a few more things for myself. I started going to the grocery store and even if I only picked up one thing, I felt that this was a help for my parents. I wanted them to know that I was trying as hard as I could to take some pressure off of them and they did make me feel good about it. I also started to go next door to their house as much as I could and do small things for my mom like wash a few dishes or clear off the table for her. As I started doing these very small things, I felt my forgiveness of myself starting to work. I felt proud of myself for the little tiny things I was doing, but to me they were huge steps.

Then I had to forgive myself for driving all of my friends and doctors crazy. I had called them so much, cried to them, and begged them to come home. I hope I did not make them feel guilty, because I did not mean to do this. I just missed everyone so much and was so lonely. I felt so bad about what I had done to Sam and did not know how to make it better. I had planned to go spend the week-end in Virginia at one time, well of course X called and I never went to see her. I never even called her to tell her I was not coming. All I could do at this point was try to make her understand that I never meant to hurt her, so I called her one day and tried to explain. Well come to find out she had planned a party for me to meet her entire family and all when I got there. I apologized whole heartedly to her and I am very lucky to this day that she has forgiven me. This just goes to show you once again how important this man was to me and how much of my power I had given up to him. I felt so guilty for hurting Sam and I am still trying to forgive myself for what I had done to her - this will be very important later.

IV

Then I had to deal with the fear of losing everything that I had worked so hard for, my career as a nurse was my main concern. I have been out of work for so long now, it is very fearful to think about what I would have to do to begin working again. I know that I will have to work hard and go into it slowly, but I know with my faith that I will be back again. I do know that I have to start getting out more and begin doing more in the public, and believe me I am trying. I miss my career so much it hurts (I know I have said this before, but it is so true). Sometimes I just sit here and wonder how long this process of healing is really going to take? If there is one thing that I am trying so hard to stress to you is that it feels like forever. The days are long, the nights are long, because you feel like you have no purpose in life. I also wonder if I really have inside of me what it is really going to take to make this happen. I always try to remember what Dr. Z. tells me and that is "Cindy, just look back to six months ago and look at how far you have come since then," this does make me feel better. Yes, I have come a long ways and I can continue.

The fear is so strong that I began to think about what my parents would do with me if I never did get better. Would I have to be put in a nursing home of something? How would any of my family ever pay for this kind of care for me? God had done so much for me by helping me get out of the black hole, but how much could I continue to ask him for? Maybe I should stop asking him for more and remember what he has already taught me and this will bring me through the healing process. Now all I have to do is learn to mix it all together and begin to let go of these fears that I have and get on with it. As Barry says "Get on with the getting on!" How much more would I have to endure, I did not know, but it was now that I would meet one of the most important people in the world to me and I would meet him in a very unique way. I had found the next person that was truly doing what they were born to do.

As I rode on my rides to the ocean so many times, I would ride around and look for a Church that I wanted to become a part of as soon as I was able to. I had thought of Folly Beach Baptist Church many times, because the ocean was such an important part of my healing process. But God had a different plan for me and he had always sent me where I needed to be and once again he did. My son had introduced my parents to Fort Johnson Baptist Church and they had been going there for about six months now. The Pastor is Schuyler Peterson (Schuyler) and everyone loved his sermons. They went to the early contemporary service with the band playing beautiful music. One day my parents came home and told me that Schuyler's sermon that morning was part one of a two part series on "Overcoming fear". Schuyler tapes his sermons and puts them on CDs, so my parents went the next day and got the CD for me to listen to. Well I listened and I could not believe my ears when I heard his words. He got it, he understood it and it was incredible to me. I did not understand how he knew so much about fear unless he had gone through it himself. Well of course this was not my concern; all I knew is that I had found my new Pastor and my new Church Family. I immediately e-mailed Schuyler and told him a little bit about me and how much his sermon was going to help me. I did not hear from him so my thoughts became confused. Then I looked back at the e-mail and realized that I had put my e-mail address in incorrectly. I e-mailed him back and told him my error and to my surprise I heard back from him that same day. He told me that he had tried many times to e-mail me back but they did not go through. He told me that he would pray for my recovery and as soon as I could come to church to please make it a point to find him and meet him. He looked forward to meeting me and getting to know me. Of course this made my day and confirmed that this was where I was supposed to be.

V

I continued on with trying to go into places and I was beginning to push myself really hard. I was having no success and this is when Dr. Z. told me I was pushing myself too hard. I could nudge myself a little bit but not to push myself. This is when he told me to look outside of his window and look at the great big oak tree in the front yard. He said to me "Cindy this tree did not grow over night," (I thought to myself, well this is great maybe when I'm 400 years old I'll be well). It scared me to slow down because I thought it would take longer for me to get there, but I did. All I ever knew was to just pray about it and I did all day and night every day and night.

I remembered at this time what Anna Marie (Marie's first grandchild) had said after Peggy died. She was about two years old and she kept telling us that Aunt Peggy was in the light. Well if Peggy was in the light then that must be where God was so this is what I did. I put a lamp on my kitchen counter and I never cut it off. Every morning when I woke up and every night when I went to sleep I started saying a prayer into the lamp so that I knew God would hear me again, but now I could see him! Thanks Anna, you will never know how much closer this made me feel to God and yes this lamp is still on today (January 2009). This gave me more strength and courage so off I went again. Please remember when I said you take three steps forward and two steps back, well I was still doing this and it was getting old. I had been sick for over a year now and it was time to get out and get on.

I started going for my rides again and trying to go into new places everyday. I just wish I could describe the feeling of panic to you the way I felt it. It is like a wave of fear like a huge bear is coming right at you and you are frozen in that one spot and you can not run and you have no voice to scream. Your heart feels like it is coming out of your chest, you cannot breathe and you begin to sweat like a pig. I also would become very dizzy and off-balance like I was going to fall down. One of the worst things in life I had to do was get in the shower. I had at one point had a severe panic attack in the shower and vowed that if I ever got out of there I would never get back in there. I was very lucky that I lived in my parent's apartment that had been built for my grandmother. The shower was built for an elderly person and had built in seats and handles everywhere. I would have to plan to get in there when my anti-anxiety meds would peak, then I would just go into panic mode and get in and hang on. I made myself get in there everyday because I was scared that if I had to go back to the hospital I did not want to stink, so I did it. I do not know how clean I got, but I did get wet, used shampoo and soap and shaved under my arms (you can laugh now).

I continued on and one day I went into Deb's pharmacy to get my meds and it began to happen. I started shaking all over and then I started to turn real red. She looked at me and was like "Cindy, do you need to sit down back here and calm down or what can I do?" I just had to leave and get to my car because that was the only way to calm it down. I got into my car and smoked my brains out, that is what worked for me. Then Dr. Z.

told me to stay inside of places and let the panic peak and then it would start to back off and you would start to calm down. I am not even going to tell you what I thought of that, I can't talk like that in this book, this is a nice book. But I did tell him "Yea right, well you go ahead and do that Jack, but I can assure you that I will not be there ok!" Some of the things I thought I can laugh at now, but I sure didn't then. I did begin to try this though and I must admit that at times it did work a little bit (I stress a little bit). But I did keep at it, for everything else Dr. Z. had told me had worked so this must be the thing to do. My trust in him is so phenomenal because I really was getting somewhere. I was not progressing at all until I started with him and I kept telling him he would never get rid of me. I'm sure he was thinking well Fred dumped her (well he didn't really dump me) to me so who can I dump her to, but he never made me feel like this (thank God for this because I am not going anywhere now).

VI

So I began to ask myself, is this coping? I thought it was, but then things started to change again and not in a good way. I began to find that there were still so many things people did not understand. Everyone thought that if I could walk into a public place, then I should be able to stay there. While I was so proud of myself for what I was doing, nobody realized how much they were hurting my feelings by saying things like this and not understanding. I once again do not know how to put into words how hard this was for me to handle, because I tried so hard to make everyone understand this is such a weird illness. Every time I start a new section of this book, I feel like this was the hardest part to go through. I could never pick the hardest, for they were all the hardest. The one thing I want everyone who reads this book to understand is that nothing was easy in any way. The state of mind we are in when we are this sick is not normal.

We feel things so differently than anyone else. I will give you a great example of this which is my daughter. She hurt my feelings everyday for a long time, but now I understand she just didn't know how to handle seeing her mother so sick. I ask myself now, how was she ever supposed to handle this? She had always had a mother for everything in her life and now her mom was gone. I know now that she missed me as much as I missed her, but I didn't know that then. I was just thinking that she didn't care about me anymore. Bless her heart and I now apologize to her if I ever made her feel bad for anything, for I never would have done that in a million years.

Boof was younger and just thought he could fix everything by saying "Come on mom just get up and let's go." So here I was wanting to die and he wanted me to put on a little black dress, color my hair, put on lipstick and go to "*Wet Willies*" with him and his friends (my first thought was, oh my God he wants me to die too)." He tried so hard to just ignore it and make it go away. When he was so sick when he was 14 years old, he almost died at that time. We had created such a strong bond all of his life due to him being so sick that he knew I would always be there for him, now I wasn't. He just wanted to fix me in the same way not understanding that surgery would not do it, only time would. He had also lost his mother.

To have to deal with all of this and try to heal would become too much very often. The fear would be so strong that the tears started and again and would not stop. Then the next great problem came along, my hormones started to kick in again. Remember that I told you that I had shut down mind, body and soul. Well I even stopped ovulating for almost a year. Well they all started coming back and with a vengeance (I almost wished I had been a man). Please do not get me wrong, I was glad that my bodily functions were coming back for that meant healing, but they were so strong that it put me into total confusion again. I was not crying from depression, for a lot of that had lifted, I was just crying. I cried if anyone looked at me wrong, told me I looked great, told me I was doing great, told me it was going to rain tomorrow, told me the sun was out, if the wrong TV show was on, if I heard the wrong song, if my cat would not come in, if I called someone and they could not talk right then (I didn't care why they could not talk, I wanted to talk), if a bill collector called, (are you getting the point)! All I can say is I cried all the time over everything! I even considered having my ovaries removed, I thought that would help. I quickly realized that this was just another mountain I had to climb, I had already climbed Mt. Everest so why not another one.

I had started sitting outside with mom and dad a little bit now and having a few meals at their house again. The neighbors would come over sometime, but I just went inside and cried more. My parents were beginning to think this was never going to end and I was never going to get better, but I tried to assure them it was ok because Dr. Z. said it was. I can't count the number of times they said "Well as long as Dr. Z. says it's ok, then it will be." They always came up with the money for Dr. Z. just so I could go there and feel better. They didn't care if he retired off of them, but he still had to take care of me.

VII

It was not long after all of this that I started laughing some. By using hypnosis I could just sit in a quiet place and let my mind wonder and calm myself down. I was becoming a pro at hypnosis and loved Karen more and more every day for this wonderful gift she had given me. So I started laughing some and then everyone thought I had really lost it. I had not laughed in so long it shocked everybody. They would look at me weird and then I would cry again. All I could think of was "What was going to be next?" These hormones did give me a little more power though, well not a little more, a lot more. I'll give you a few examples: A lady at the IRS told me that if I didn't have a way to make my payments, maybe I could pawn my tv or something to make a payment. My response to that was "When you get home tonight lady this is what I want you to do with your TV" (I will stop that story there). Then I was having problems getting disability after a year. I had great attorneys, but now it was in the hands of the government, so I figured if this was the case then I would go to the government. I called the Governor of SC and in three weeks I received my disability.

Then I had to deal with the bill collectors calling me at least 10-15 times a day. Well one day I got really mad, for I had explained my situation to them a million times and assured them that they would be paid as soon as I went back to work and that I understood that I owed about $60,000.00 in medical bills, but they didn't care and they never stopped calling. I then picked my phone up one day and called my phone company and had all my numbers changed to unlisted. Wow the phones stopped ringing and it was so quiet (I showed them huh)! You know it's kind of like you are not allowed to get sick in this country unless you are a millionaire. I was a travel nurse and had lost my insurance four weeks after I got sick so I had sixteen hospital visits and many doctor visits with no money. It's a shame that my parents had to use their house that they had worked for thirty years for to get enough money to support us all, which made me wonder what do people that do not have these resources do? I would have ended up homeless and on the streets or in a shelter. I was so blessed to have been given the people in my life that I had been given.

VII

It was now around the beginning of August 2008 and I felt the need more and more to go to God's house and thank him personally for all that he had given me. I knew I would be safe there so I decided that I would go with my parents, but I would only go for the sermon. That way I would be there for about

30 minutes and maybe I could stay for that long. I had to miss the band playing, but music was still pretty hard for me to listen to, but that was ok. I knew God would understand what time I could give him and he would be proud of me. So I made my plan and I planned my morning out. Of course I cried for two days and the entire morning before I left for my first church sermon at my new church. Then of all things to find my parents I had to go up to the balcony. I had been scared of heights all of my life, but I knew God was with me so we walked up those steps together. I cried the whole time I listened to Schuyler and hardly remember the sermon, but I was there and it felt great.

After the sermon I stayed to meet Schuyler and I was shaking like a leaf. I had been there for about 40 minutes, but I was going to meet him and I did. I introduced myself to him and he did remember me. He said he was glad to see that I had made it and if there was anything he could do to help me all I had to do was let him know. Then he gave me a big hug, I left and cried for two days. These were happy tears and I loved every one of them. This began my new life with my new church family and I could not wait for Sundays to come. It became my special day to give thanks by going to God's house. I had also run into a lot of old friends that I had not seen for years and this was great. I knew I always had someone to hold onto even if mom and dad were not there. Being there gave me peace and calmness that I had not felt for a long time, so I decided to join this church on October 18, 2008. My mom and dad had left early so they missed it. I would have loved for them to have been there, but I just felt this power over me, got up walked down that isle to Schuyler grabbed onto him and asked if I would be welcome there as a member. He told me that would be a wonderful thing and welcomed me with opened arms. I was introduced to the congregation and had found my new home. Yes I was crying my eyes out, but was very happy at this moment.

I began to talk to Schuyler more about my illness that I was going through and asked him if he would baptize me again. I wanted to renew my faith in God and wash away all my sins. He was thrilled and we did the baptism on November 9, 2008. I wore the diamond ring of my grandmothers that my daughter will be married with, the necklace with the nursing symbol on it that Sam had given me for graduation from nursing school. I wanted these things blessed in the holy water for they were very special to me. To this day I have still not washed the shorts and t-shirt I wore under the robe and I never will. This date November 9, 2008 will always be my second birthday and it will be celebrated as such. Even though there is not a lot that I can contribute to my new church family at this time, I know that one day I will and this will be a joyous time for me.

VIII

There are a few things that I really want you to take from this chapter that are very important to me. Dealing with guilt is always hard, fear is fear that is so severe at time it can debilitate your life and hurt feelings and crying are all just a part of the healing process from this kind of mental shut down. I was very lucky that my mom and dad made sure that I always had the best health care that was possible. I understand that a lot of people do not believe in hypnosis (I didn't either), but I will tell you that it has turned out to be one of the best things that I have ever done. The main thing it taught me was how to learn to let things go! Yes, just let things go! It gives you a sense of peace and calmness, because you can take yourself out of any situation and put yourself into a safe place. It takes a long time to learn how to do this, but practice does make perfect.

People always tell me, oh Cindy, it's just all in your head. Well yes, that is where your brain and mind are and they are what are sick, so ignore statements like this. Remember that this can happen to anyone at anytime and you are not alone. You will learn how to help people understand what they can do for you, although this will take a very long time, because you will not even know what you need. I only hope that some of the things I did can help you and the people caring for you, that's my goal.

At this time I am still trying to get out more and more, no matter how hard it is. I can go in to places for about 15 minutes now without panic kicking in and believe it or not I can stay a few minutes when it does kick in. I am much steadier on my feet and no longer use a walker. I laugh a lot now and enjoy life a lot more. I am still scared to sleep on my right side and I do not think that I ever will get over this, but we will see. I do sleep better though and I have more hope every day that this will end and my healing process will be over. I want to go back to my life so bad and be a nurse again. I know in my heart and soul it will all come (I will get in that shower again and be comfortable if it kills me), *I just have to wait like that oak tree did, continue to grow and I will...*

CHAPTER FIVE

Caregivers
(The Purpose)

I

Well I finally got to the main purpose of this book and that is to help people learn how they can help others who find themselves as sick as I have been. They may not have had a situation like mine, but the illness is the same. You may find yourself taking care of a loved one, a friend or anyone else that is close to you. There are so many things that I did not understand that I needed from others until much later in the healing process. At the time of my illness, I was so sick I did not care what others did or did not do for me and I did not know what I needed. *Now I do!*

I can look back through my journals and find that many times when I needed something, I was just too scared to ask them for more so I didn't. My mom and dad or the rest of my family had never gone through anything like this before and did not understand what was wrong with me or what to do with me. Believe me this is not their fault, they just did not know and most people don't. They all did such a wonderful job and sacrificed all they had for my recovery and this I will never be able to thank them enough for. They tried so hard to understand, but they were just as frustrated as I was. They could not see any progress for such a long time and this scared them a lot. I must say they were troopers in every way.

Since my purpose in life is to help others, I believe that I can help a lot of sick people by giving their caregivers some tips on what I have now learned of what I needed from mine. I say to you all that it will be a long road as you take care of someone so sick, but just believe that it will one day be over and you will all find peace again. I will begin with the beginning for me and this is for you, *the caregivers*!

II

When someone goes through such a traumatic unexpected event the first things they do is cry and get very panicked. They will cry their eyes out 24 hours a day and there is nothing you will be able to do to stop it. These are tears that are non-stoppable; they bring fear to them which leads to panic in a very serious way. A shock to the system shuts down the central nervous system and emotions become very weird. Tears are a very normal emotion and they have never hurt anyone. You must try very hard to not let them know that you are sad for them, just accept the tears as normal. It will become very hard for you to see them so upset all the time and there is nothing you can do about it, but there are a few things that you can do to make them feel better (it will also make you feel better, knowing you are helping them). You can give them a cold rag to put on their eyes, for they become very sore. My daughter brought me a Mary Kay product called *Indulge* which is a soothing eye gel. This worked great for me and I used just about the whole jar of it. You can also get them moisturizing eye drops which also help a lot, my mom made sure I had plenty of this.

The fear will kick in about this time and panic attacks may begin. This will be the most frightening thing that they will ever go through and they are no fun to watch. You will have no idea what to do for them, my parents called 911 and got me to the emergency room. This is when the worst part of my illness began. I could handle the tears, but not the panic attacks. I explained earlier how you feel when you are having one, but I can not stress enough how fearful they are. They kept telling me at the ER that nobody had ever died from a panic attack, so I knew I was going to be the first. Mine were so bad I would have them in my sleep and wake up screaming with fear. The only way to calm me was to go to the hospital and get intravenous Ativan and then go home and sleep. But the worst part was waiting for the next one to come; you know it is going to happen so you just live in fear of them.

The most important thing I have learned that you can do is try your hardest to remain calm through these times. They will feel your calmness and this will help a lot. Talk to them in a low voice and tell them to breathe slowly and keep telling them it will be over soon. When the attack calms stay with them while they go to sleep, this will make them feel safe and not alone. I cannot stress how much they need to feel safe.

III

This is when all the meds start to come into play. Psychiatric meds are very hard to take and they can make you very sick. They made me feel like my head was in one room and my body was in the other. They made me nauseated, gave me terrible headaches and at times even hallucinations. The doctors kept changing them, but it seemed that I would never find the ones that I would be able to tolerate. This is going to be a hard time for you because you are going to have to change meals around a lot. There will be very few foods they will be able to eat and tolerate. My mom made me hot tea all the time and this really helped a lot, she never ran out and made plenty of it. My mom had to cook for them at their house and different foods for me which I know must have exhausted her. I was lucky that I lived in their apartment next door to them. They were close to me which was a very big help for them.

I was back in the hospital twice due to allergic reactions from two of the meds (this can happen with a lot of them). The worst part was the dizziness and the unsteadiness which I was led to believe was from the meds. Some meds can cause these side effects, but panic can cause them too. I found out later that mine were from panic, but this was not until after I was off of a lot of the meds because I just could not tolerate them. It becomes a game of terror and hell and you eventually begin to question which one would be better.

IV

One thing you will need to do is get help from other family members. Call in everyone that is available to help. My sister was a huge help to me and my family at this time. She would come and sit with me at times which would give my mom a break. She would also go to the hospital with me and sit so that my mom and dad could stay home at times. Heather would come at times, but she never stayed long, we know now the reason for that. But it was a comfort to me when she was there. Boof would come at times, but he ran like lightning after about five minutes. Everyone has to chip in and do their share at times of tragedy. Do not be scared to ask for help, for it is their responsibility too. You will become exhausted quickly, but just remember in 50 years nobody will care that you did not vacuum or dust the house, these things can wait.

What will take up a lot of your time is just sitting with the sick one. Spend as much time as you can with them, hold onto them and continue to tell them this will end soon. They need lots of hugs and people to hold onto. They need people to give them hope and they need this from you, for you are the closest person to them. I could not wait until morning would come because my mom would bring her coffee and cigarettes to my apartment and sit with me and have coffee time. She had a chair at the end of my bed so she could be right next to me when I could not get out of the bed. This was the most special time we had together and when it was over I would cry my eyes out waiting for her to come back (I am crying right now just thinking about these times).

I knew she had to go away because she left to go fix my breakfast and do the things she had to do at her house. But that did not matter; I wanted her with me all the time. I remember thinking how great it would be if I could cut her into threes and have three of her. It sounds so selfish of me now to talk about the way I felt, but believe me I did not realize it then. They say it does not matter how old you get, when you get sick you always want mama. There has never been a more true statement than this! Dad would come back to see me sometimes, but it freaked him out as much as Boof. He did try as hard as he could, but he didn't have any idea what to do for me. I think now that this scared him more than anyone else. But to me I know he tried his best and that is all that anyone can do. You never know how people are going to react in a given situation until they are faced with it, and I sure gave it to them completely.

V

It was around this time that they can become very suicidal. I did not want to live another day with the pain and loneliness that I felt. This is a time where the caregiver will become very confused. To hear the words from your loved one that they want to die is never a good thing to have to go through. This is when you will learn more than ever how to remain calm, and repeat over and over to them that this will be ok (these two little letters can have a huge meaning to a suicidal person). You must remember that this person has lost all hope now and this is when they will need you the most. My mom has never been a very huggy and touchy person, but I would imagine in my head that she was lying next to me and holding me. It's not her fault she did not have these traits, they are genetic and nobody in her family has them. But that was ok; she made up for it in all other ways. The important part is that I could feel her and I knew she was there. So give hugs and give lots of them, hold their hand, and just touch them. The sense of touch is one of the strongest emotions that humans have and this is when they are needed the most. Do not worry you will never run out of hugs, they are plentiful and sent from above.

VI

This next part is one of the most important parts of this book that I will ever write, so please read carefully! When someone is suicidal all they are interested in doing is making their plan and going through with it. You may not even know what they are doing in their mind, but there are some triggers that will help you realize what they are doing. Some of the things I did were to tell everyone that I was ok now and they could go back to their house, so all of a sudden I wanted to be alone. I knew that if I could get rid of them I could go through with my plan. After a while you forget about them finding you later or anything like that, you just want it over. Another sure sign is that their mood will change because they know that this is about to be over, watch carefully for this, for I know mine did. I would go into the living room more and try to make them believe that I was having a good day. You will start to feel more comfortable with them now because you are starting to feel like they are getting better, but believe me they are not.

84

When you start to see these signs, begin to think that something is not right. If they tell you to go ahead and go out for awhile: *DO NOT GO*! This is the time when you may have to put them in the hospital for safety. They will tell you no that they are ok, but do not believe them. You now have to really take charge and keep them safe. You know that it is not possible for you to stay with them every second of every day and nobody is ever expected to, that is just not possible. I was hospitalized three times for suicidal ideations and this is how my parents kept me safe. I thank them now, but I sure didn't then. I thought that if I promised them that I would not hurt myself they would believe me and they did. Now I am telling you to never believe their promises, they will promise you the world and it is a lie. They just want to get on with their plan. I was very lucky that my plan never worked and I know now why which I have already told you, but not everyone looks for healing in the same way I did, so they may not be so lucky.

VII

This is a time when your sick person may start to give you a hard time, you will not let them go through with their plan and they are getting pissed off. Their frustrations are going to be taken out on you, because you are the closest person to them. The best thing you can do is ignore them and continue to tell them that they will get over these feelings in time. Remind them over and over again that frustration is normal and it is ok for them to rant and rave. What my mom did was just change the subject and start to talk about other things. Believe it or not this did calm me down a lot! She just refused to put up with that non-sense and changed it. She would even get my dad in there and the tone in his voice would stop me quickly. I hurt their feelings at times like this and after all they were doing for me. Believe me they were not being mean or anything, it was just their way of handling the situation as they found it. I can see now that when I became frustrated and took it out on them, their frustration only became stronger. Believe me we had our times of anger at each other. I will quote a passage from one of my journals, this is dated November 14, 2007. I wrote "I do not know why my mom is being so mean to me now. Why doesn't anyone understand that they should just let me go if that is what I want to do. I am 48 years old and they are treating me like a child. I am getting sick of both of them (mom & dad) and I just wish they would go away. I am able to make my own decisions and I have chosen to end my life. I will do it no matter what they say and they can stick me in any hospital they want, but I will get out and do it! So just go away and leave me alone!" As I read this now it makes me sick to my stomach. But you must remember and I will probably remind you of this many times, they do not know what they are doing or what they are thinking. They do not mean to be treating you this way, it's just the illness. Believe me they will feel guilty later and then they will have to deal with this, but that was already written.

VIII

I have talked about loneliness a lot in this book, but now I want to tell you what you can do to help with that. I mentioned that there could be 20 people in the room with me, but I never felt anyone. This is one of the saddest things that this person will have to go through. Loneliness brings boredom that is also horrible. There is nothing that they can do because they are too sick. I could not watch TV, listen to music, read, or even walk in the yard. Any kind of noise made me very dizzy and more unbalanced, so all I could do was sit or lay there.

I keep mentioning that they need people with them and this is very true. When you have to leave them remind them that you will be right back and not to worry. Tell them that you will be back in about five minutes and they will believe you, even if you know it will be longer than that. This will also take them out of the position to hurt themselves. Remind them they are not alone and you are just a call away. My mom and dad even had a buzzer rigged up by my bed so all I had to do was push it and it buzzed at their house. If I did buzz it believe me they came a running. I was wired for sound in every way. I think I over did the buzzer though, because that was the first thing they took out when I started getting better.

Another thing you can do for them is make sure they have plenty of notebooks and pens, so they will have something to do. They can write letters, keep a journal or just write about how they are feeling. This does help them a lot, I know because it sure did help me. My mom also got me coloring books, crayons and paint sets. Believe me I colored and painted a lot, they weren't real good and they are now in the garbage, but I loved them at the time. Another good thing you can do for them is read to them. Start a good book, we never did this because I have to read for myself. But it may work well for your sick person. This is also very time consuming and you may find that you do not have the time for it, but maybe someone else that comes over can take some time for this.

IX

I have mentioned that I would never turn this into a religious book, but it is the way that I found recovery. I would never have gotten out of the black hole if I would not have found God and put him into my heart. He brought me all the strength and courage I needed to keep on working, therefore; I got out. You may find that this will also help your sick person. You can talk to them about God and the power that he holds (and I do mean power). Talking about God to them and using the tools that I used may bring them hope and peace of one day recovery from this awful time. I had William at Palmetto introduce God back into my life and I will never be able to thank him enough. Since I have found God again in my life, I know that I will live the rest of my life for him. I will welcome the tasks that he sends for me to do with open arms and I will do them to the best of my ability. This brings great peace and comfort to me every day as I still continue to recover. I know that everyone is not religious and I will never judge people for how they live their lives, this is just a suggestion for them that I know is what brought me healing. It is a choice that each person has to make. My parents had not been to church in many, many years, but when I got sick they found peace and comfort there. They are now joining the church also and finding God as I did. This brings me great joy and happiness and I know they will feel better every day and love life more.

I find now that this brought them hope that I would get well and become the person that I was, only better. Sometimes in our lives we find that the way we are living needs changes and this may be one. You as a caregiver will be very worried about your loved one that is why I am including this portion into my book. This can also bring you peace and hope as it did for my caregivers. It is incredible how you are led in the right direction as we were and that may be any direction that comes your way. Any way can be right for you as long as it brings the same results.

X

A very important thing that you can do is remind your sick person that they have to find strength and courage from their guts. When they start to give up remind them that they have to find strength and courage and when they can no longer find more, remind them to dig deeper and deeper, they will find more. When I talk about coming from our guts, I mean our guts. Strength and courage are buried very deep and is very hard to find, but it is there.

It is the gift that we get from above and there is one place you will find it. I will now take you to the place were I found it. It was the ocean._ When I was at my worst part of my illness, my dad would drive me to the ocean almost every day. The ocean was given to us from God for healing and it does. Tell the person that "When the tide goes out it will take their illness out with it and when the ocean comes in it will bring wellness to them." As I was able to drive at times, I was always led to the ocean. I didn't know why then - but once again I do now. There is really not a more peaceful place on this earth which can bring such serene calmness. This is something you can do to get them out of the house and believe me they need to get out. They need to know that the world is still going on around them and they will begin to feel like they are still in the world.

When the time comes for them to start going into places, start them out by going with them. They will not be able to go by themselves and it helps them to hear from you that this is ok. Do not expect them to stay long, for just walking in for them will be a huge step. If they start to panic, you can calm them down by letting them hold onto you. I cannot tell you how many times I have just grabbed onto people out of the blue. Thank goodness I was with people I knew, or others would have gotten grabbed just like they did. I would have had a lot of explaining to do in that situation. Could you just imagine being somewhere and a stranger just grab onto you? If this ever does happen to you, now you will know a reason that it could possibly happen.

XI

You as the caregiver must also remember to take care of yourself. My mom used to kiss me goodnight every night at about 7:00p.m. (that's when I went to bed) and she would tell me she would see me in the morning, but if I needed her just use my buzzer. I know this must have been a huge relief to go home and just relax for awhile, but she also had all of her stuff to do. (She tells me now that it was like putting a baby to bed and going yeah!) I do not know to this day how she did it all, but she did. My dad helped out at their house by cooking a lot and cleaning. I know now that this was his way of helping and he did a great job. I am so proud of both of them and everyone that was there to help out at any time. My mom and dad did all the physical stuff and Sharon handled all the emotional stuff. Bless her heart she was going through so much at the time with her mother-in-law (nana) being so sick and then me getting so sick. I really do not know to this day how she did not just lose it the same way I did. We are all very grateful that Sharon did not have to work outside of the home, but believe me she became a nurse in every sense of the word. I wrote her a poem one night that I would like to share with you now. Please remember I am not a poet and I was on strong meds:

WHAT IS A NURSE
They say a nurse has a uniform and a card
that says I'm someone big,
but now I know a nurse is a person
with compassion, love and care.

One thing I never knew before was I thought
our family only had one, but now I
know deep in my heart
we were really blessed with two.

I often wonder when I sit alone,
what would Nana and I have done, if
we would not have had nurse Sharon
at our side to love us all the time.
So thank yourself everyday,
for that's what I'm trying to say,
for now I know the meaning of the word
"nurse," it's you in every way.

(June 11, 2008)

One very important thing you can do for them is help them get financial help from the government. There are a lot of great programs out there, I know it takes a long time for the system to work, but it takes away a lot of guilt from the sick person when they are able to contribute financially again. My mom helped me fill out a lot of paperwork and helped with my attorneys. You do not need money for an attorney, because they only get paid if you do get disability, so do not worry about that financial burden.

Try to be patient with the people that are working for your case for there are a lot of sick people out there and they are very busy. The Department of Social Services also has a lot of programs that will help, just call them and they will send you lots of information. They are very nice to work with and really seem to care about your well-being. Try to work with the hospitals if you loose your insurance, they love to harass you for money, but just don't let it get to you. Remember that if you have no money, they can't get any money. I know that one day they will be paid and I wish it was now. But that is not possible so I just go on and try to forget it.

As I end this chapter for you; the caregivers, please remember your sick person will never die from a panic attack or tears. The only thing and main thing that you have to watch for is suicide, *for this will kill them*. I say a prayer every day for anybody in this given situation and I hope for the best for all of you. Just take it slow and remember it will be a long recovery for everyone and you may not think you are doing a good job, but you are. They are very lucky to have somebody to love them and care for them as I did. I think back now to the worst of times for me and all I can say is that I wish my parents, children, family and friends would have realized at the time what a huge help they all were to me.

As my recovery progresses I still live in fear every day that my life will never be the same as it was before my illness. I work so hard every day and sometimes I feel like I am getting nowhere. I pray everyday that I will be able to be a nurse again and a great mother, daughter, sister and friend to all the people in my life. I am so thankful for the disability that I now receive from the government, because I will never have to be in fear of my parents losing everything to take care of me. But believe me I would rather be working and having a life back. I know in my heart this will all happen in time. Like I have said I do not like to wait for things, but I am learning.

I hope this will be a help to you all and I wish you all the best!

As I began to heal and start to want to live again, I began to realize all of the things in life that I had learned, that I never knew before. I learned hard lessons and easy lessons, but they were all lessons that I will take with me forever through the rest of my life. I want to share them with you for a few reasons, they are just great lessons and they may help you in your recovery. We all need to continue learning every day to grow, so I hope my lessons will help you. Please remember that I had always lived my life in such high gear that I never knew what slowing down was, *but now I do…*

Notes

Notes

Notes

Notes

Notes

Notes

Notes

Notes

Notes

Notes

CHAPTER SIX

My Lessons Learned

The only thing I can say as I start this chapter is that I thought I knew a lot in life. I have lived for almost fifty years now (a half a century) and have come to the conclusion that I knew nothing about the true things in life. I was getting by and living a good life, but little did I know what life was really all about. During my illness and beginning of my recovery I have now realized that there were many things I needed to learn to live a better life. I learned hard lessons, easy lessons, confusing lessons, but all are   lessons that I will take with me for the rest of my life. I am including these lessons in hopes of helping people to become stronger and healthier, in hopes that they will never have to go through what I did. I know now that by learning the things that I have, that I will be well one day and I will never let this happen to me again (this I can promise you).

I know that I had no control over my illness happening, but by being weak and not knowing these things in life, I know that I contributed to allowing this to happen to me. Believe me this hurts to have to admit this, but it is so true; therefore, I will share my lessons with you and maybe they will make you stronger as they did for me.

This chapter was written at Folly Beach sitting in my car at the wash-out. I was looking at the ocean and the words just came to me from the water. I took out a sheet of paper and a pen and started writing what God was saying to me. It was January 15, 2009 at 10:30 a.m. and it was 23 degrees on a very sunny day, the ocean was very calm. I sat there for about an hour and that was as long as it took for all of my lessons learned to come to light. So we will start with lesson #1 and there will be many...

1. GOD: All of my life I had always thought of God as just being there for me for anything that I ever needed. I had always prayed every night and given thanks for all that he had given me and prayed for peace in the world. I had mentioned before that this was all I thought I had to do to be loved by him and have him in my life, but I never really knew until now the true power of God and what peace and comfort he could bring to me. But now I have learned the real lesson and truth about finding God and truly living my life for him. The worst thing I had done in my life was question God about why he did things like take my best friend from me at 22 years of age, how he could take Peggy from us all at such a young age? I understood that my grandparents were supposed to die for they had lived long wonderful lives and yes death is a part of life. I also know that I will have to live through the death of many more of my loved ones when they are elderly and die because it is their time. I questioned the violence in the world, how people could just kill each other for no reasons that made sense to me? I questioned why babies were abused by their very own parents and he let this happen? I questioned why drugs were taking over the world and killing such young kids? The main thing I had to learn was that God gives us each a journey, but he also gives us a brain to make our own choices. It is up to each of us to make our journeys what we want them to be. So I had to learn that "God is there with me, but only when I truly found him and put him in my heart and made the commitment to live my life for him and his

people." Now that I have found this, I have found that things are becoming wonderful for me. I know that I still have a long recovery to go, but now it is ok. I have learned a phrase from God and it is "Unshakable faith." I now know that there is nobody in this world that can ever take my faith from me now no matter what the situation is. I know now that God will never leave me again and will always be watching over me. I know that I now live my life for him and will do any task that he sends for me and I will do it the best in every way that I can. This lesson is the best thing that I could have ever learned in my life. I would love to pass it on to each one of you, but you are the one that must want it as much as I did. This was my way of beginning my healing process and as I have said may not be for everyone. But I will spread God's word now to anyone who wants to listen. It is my greatest lesson in life!

2. MY CHILDREN: I do not think I could ever count all of the lessons I have learned from my children, Heather and Boof, but I know there are many. They have taught me a love that is truly unconditional no matter what. I will start with Heather because she was first, but not more important. Heather is 26 years old now and becoming a beautiful young woman. She has a mind of her own and she sure does use it. Her imagination has taught me that there is nothing in this world that you could possibly dream about and not make it happen. She loves life and definitely lives it to the fullest. This tells me that if she can do it then I can too. She is the one that taught me to listen to the ocean and it will talk to you and yes it does. But the most important thing she taught me is to be yourself and never change for anything or anybody. She taught me to be independent, for there is no body more independent than her. Boof has taught me lessons that I also needed to learn. He is now 22 years old, he went through an illness

that almost cost him his life also, but he remained strong and made it through as a perfect healthy person. He has also taught me forgiveness which is very important to me now. I have had to forgive him for breaking my heart many times through his teenage years, but he also lives his life in his own way. This taught me to make my own choices and live my life my way. He taught me to love someone no matter what they end up doing to you and now I have learned to do this. I thank God every day that he has made it through all of the hard times he has gone through and am very glad that he is finally growing up and learning a good life (well trying to). My faith in him is so strong that there is no way he will not become a wonderful man, a good husband and father one day, his life will be great. The lessons my children have taught me will be with me forever and have been a huge part of my recovery. I do tell them I love them every day that I can and every night as I go to sleep. Please always remember and never forget both of you that "There ain't no mountain high enough, there ain't no valley low enough, there ain't no river wide enough to ever keep me from getting to you, just holler and I will feel your needs and nothing will ever be able to stop me from getting to you." Thanks you two!

3. MY FAMILY: When I talk about my family, I include them all. The lessons they have all taught me are priceless. A lot of people in this world do not understand what having a true family that sticks together no matter what can actually be like. I never knew this about my family until I became very ill. When I got sick everyone showed up to help me and take care of all of my needs, no matter what they were. This taught me what a family can truly be. My family had been broken at times, but that did not matter in any way when one of us needed the others. I cannot stress enough how we all came together through these times. I had always wanted a true family to raise my

children, and even though their father and I were divorced we still stuck together and raised our children. When I think now about lessons learned about families, I only wish to say to each of you to appreciate yours, for I have sure learned to appreciate mine. I do tell them I love them every day or every chance I get.

4. LOVE: This may be hard for you to understand, but after I got hurt so badly and became so ill, I realize now that I am the lucky one (not him). I got the chance to learn to truly love a man which I had never had before. I was lucky enough to finally find and have the gift of love that not everybody on this earth has the opportunity to have. I learned that it was ok to be myself and be comfortable with someone in every way. I learned emotions that I never knew existed and I learned to love the ocean even more than I ever thought I could. I learned to have fun in any given situation, just make everything fun. I wish I could tell you all the fun things I did, but that would not be appropriate at this time. Now I have learned to turn all the pain into happy memories and let go of the pain. I know that I will never forget X, but I know now that I can live without him. I no longer need him, for I have found in myself what love truly is and it is to love myself. I will always thank him for that. Love is another gift from above and it can truly change your life, for it sure did mine. I have always loved all people equally no matter what. It never mattered to me where they were from, what their life was, or what their past was, for they are all the same to me. Everyone is my brother or sister and I have enough love for all. I have never judged anyone, for that is not my job, I think this is the reason I am such a wonderful nurse and person. This is love!

5. BLESSINGS: If I sat here tonight and listed all the blessings in my life, I would be writing for months. My greatest blessing is that I am alive and get to live on this

beautiful earth and share it with all the ones I love. I have been blessed to live through the worst of times and am now coming through to the other side. I remember when I did not want to live any longer and now all I want to do is live. Now that is a blessing. I have been blessed with all of the greatest things in life and it doesn't get any better than that!

6. OCEAN:If you want to go to the most beautiful place on earth and learn all the lessons I have learned, all you have to do is go to the ocean. I have talked a lot about the ocean in this book as a huge part of my healing process. I talked to the ocean and got all the answers to all of my questions and this is how I learned all my lessons. Believe me I listened to the ocean, yes to every word it said. I was desperate for lessons and I was lucky to know where to go. As I asked for faith, I found it; as I asked for strength, I got it; as I asked for courage, I got it; as I asked for healing, I got it; as I asked for love, I got it; as I asked for confidence, I got it; as I asked for laughter again, I got it; as I asked for my heart to open again and heal, I got it; as I asked to find my soul again, I found it. The ocean took away all the bad and brought me all the good stuff back. The ocean can be calm and it can be fierce. I learned that the ocean talks to me more when it is calm and peaceful. I have a bottle of the ocean sitting on my counter and every time I want the ocean I have it. I took a bottle of the ocean to Fred also as a gift of his helping me so much and caring so much about me and my wellness. I had told him that if I could ever get out of my car and walk to the ocean, I would fill us up bottles of the water and take one to him. I will never forget the look on his face when I took him that bottle of water. I wrote a note on it to keep it on his desk and if he ever needed God, that is where he could find him. He was so proud of me that I had done it. *It was huge!* I can find answers at any time I need them, just by going into

the kitchen. Yes, all the lessons I ever needed to learn, I found them there. That is why there is so much water on this earth, enough for healing everyone!

7. POWER:I saved power for #7 because this is my lucky number; both my children and I were born in the 7th month (July). I have never won anything using this number, (not that I do not try, I play the lottery every week using 7 & 11), but I sure did learn the lesson of having and keeping my power. I learned that if you lose your power or give it away, you have lost your sense of self. You lose all your control over your entire life; this is when you truly become lost. When I lost my power I fell into the deep black hole. When I got my power back, I began to find my way out. I learned that my power is myself, I will try to explain what I mean. I found inside of myself that I was lost and could not find my world. As I found that my power was the answer, then I was able to find the ways to begin my release from this terrible feeling of being lost. It was through my power that I found all of my lessons, my blessings and my hope. This is how I got my recovery started. I do know now that I will never lose my power again no matter what - you will see why soon!

8. HOPE:Since I have never really understood the meaning of the word hope, I looked up the definition. It means: "To want or expect something: to have a wish to get or do something or for something to happen or be true, especially something that seems possible or likely." When I think of this in my life I can find the lessons that I needed to learn. I have never expected anything from anyone or never wanted anyone to expect something from me. Was I wrong, I guess I was! I knew that it was ok to want things, but you had to work for them to get them. I did not have to learn to wish for things, but what I didn't realize that my wishes had to be for things that were possible or likely. I wished for whatever I wanted to happen in my life and

the lives of the people I loved, so this was a huge lesson. Now I have learned what true hope is and I sure do have it. I hope for many things every day, but now I know that my hopes are possible, because I know what to hope for. I have a lot of hope for everyone and everything and now I know my hopes will come true.

9. TRUST:This is when I learned to trust my gut. Now I listen to my gut and it gives me the answer of who to trust and who not to. I did lose my sense of trust when I was hurt by someone that I trusted so much, but I have learned to not let him take that away from me. I will trust in someone again as I do many others. I know what to look for in a person that is truth and what is a lie. What a lesson we all need to know. Trust to me is not a feeling it is shown in the actions and persona of a person. By listening to a person talk about their life, you can also tell if this is someone you can trust. I really needed to learn this lesson a lot. See I always trusted everyone until they proved me differently, now they have to prove their trust to me first. Trust to me is also the truth now. Now, let's go there…

10. HONESTY: I have always felt that if you do not have honesty, you have nothing. I have never in this life had a reason to lie to anyone about anything. I learned a huge lesson though, because everyone does not feel this way. When I look back to my relationship with X, I find now that he lived his life in lies. He lied to himself and everyone else; it was his way of life. Yes, I knew it but, like they say "Love is blind," well it is. If I would have allowed myself to see the lies, I would not have let this happen to me, I would have left. I also learned that little white lies are different than true lies. During my illness I found myself telling my mom and dad little white lies to try to make them feel better and relax some. For example: I was smoking a lot at that time (I mean a lot) and they were buying my cigarettes which cost a lot. They were

worried about my health and would try their hardest to try to get me to cut down some, but I just couldn't. So I would get Sharon to bring me cigarettes and I would hide them. This way they thought I was doing better even though I wasn't. This is what I call a little white lie and told for a good reason, but I know now it was wrong. The truth does always set you free. I never told them this either, so I guess they will know this now too. My biggest lesson I learned here is that I feel terrible about lying at all, especially to my mom and dad of all people. I know now that I will never lie again no matter what, not even if it is for the right reason, because there is no right reason.

11. FRIENDSHIP: This is a part of my book that I really love, because my friends are so important to me and such a wonderful part of my life. I am one of these people that when you become a friend of mine, you are a friend for life. I still have the people in my life that I knew in middle and high school. I was going to add this section in my family section, because they are so much my family, but I decided to give them their own spot. What I have learned from them is pure and simple dedication, people who I can share all my secrets with, they always understand no matter what my life is going through at the time and they never leave me to be alone when I need them. Wow, what great lessons are these! When I wrote the dedication to this book, I included the friends that have been in my life the longest and the most. But I do have a lot of other friends that are also very special to me and they know who they are. I have also learned recently the sadness of losing a friend because they no longer want to be in my life. Even though he doesn't want me in his life, believe me I will always keep him in mine. I just don't know how to let a friend go! I know that in the last two years, I have worn out all of my friends, just as I have my family. I know that when it's 22 degrees outside, 8:30 at night and

they say they were just leaving to go shopping, that they are not. But it's ok. I know they just have to have a break sometimes. I am sick of my whining too, so I just talk to the computer and keep on writing. I will always remember all the great times with Rosie, Marie, Sam, Linda and Barry like they were yesterday. Of course we have also had sad times, but life does go on. My greatest lesson here is to begin to be a better person to my friends and let them know how important they are to me. I promise you all that as my recovery advances, I will be less whiny and more fun!

12. APPRECIATION: What a huge word with a huge meaning! As I think of appreciation, I realize that I really did not take the time to appreciate anything the way I should have. The small things or the big things, I guess I just figured they would be there no matter what, well did I learn a lesson here! I think it would be fair to say that I just took things for granted (he kids would be fine, my family would be fine, friends would be fine, and the sun would always come up tomorrow). When I got so sick, I no longer had any control over anything that happened in my life or anyone else's. When I think of this now, I can honestly say I will never take anything for granted again and I do appreciate everything in my life. When I sit and look around me, I see things that I have never seen before and I look at them in a very different way. I love to watch the sun come up now in the mornings, I love it when it rains and washes the entire world, I love to listen to the birds sing (and yes they are singing to me), I love to watch the flowers bloom, have you ever really appreciated the beauty in the flowers when they smell so fresh? Colors seem so much brighter to me, I guess that's why I have a yellow and purple porch now. But the things I have learned to appreciate the most are the people in my life, my God, my children, my family, my friends, my patients

that I will one day take care of again, my church family and pastor, and of course the ocean. I have also learned to appreciate the field of Psychology so much more and appreciate the people that give their time to help people in my situation. As I look back to my Palmetto days and remember how sick I was, I cannot believe that these poor people had to put up with people like me. Even though we do not understand how demanding and needy we are, I am telling you now we are. I have also thought a lot about the way mental health care needs to change in this country - this I will go into later in another chapter. I only hope that everyone there knows how much I appreciated them, if they didn't know then now they do! I have also learned that I had to learn to slow down to learn to appreciate the simple things in life, no matter how big or small. I now take the time to enjoy my coffee in the mornings, I do stop and pick up trash as I walk down the street, I enjoy what God has given to me on this earth that he created for me, all you have to do is look around you and you will see it too!

13. PATIENCE: Well look here, number 13 and guess what, its patience. The one thing in life that I have had the hardest time learning and believe me it has not gotten any easier. I am beginning to believe that you have to be born with it to have it. I know my mom has it, my dad does not, and my kids, well forget it. Have you ever heard the phrase "Self gratification now!" This phrase is Heather, Boof and me. I am sorry kids if you got this from me, but take it from me and start trying to learn it now because you will sure need it later. So, I have learned to slow down, I have learned to appreciate, does this mean that I am learning patience? I am not sure so I looked the word up and got the meaning, it is "The ability to endure waiting, delay or provocation without being annoyed or upset; or to preserve calmly when faced with difficulties." Oh now I

understand, this must be a word other than English, see I only speak English. No wonder I don't get it! Endure waiting, why should I have to wait for something and to not get annoyed or upset while waiting and I thought I was crazy? I think this is just a stupid word and I don't think I will put it in my dictionary. But you know that I have to. If I want to get well, I have to learn patience and learn how to practice it. Remember that oak tree, yeah well I do and I think about it all the time. It is a pretty tree and it did take a long time to grow to its beauty, but I am almost 50 years old. I often wonder if I will live long enough to grow that beauty. I must now get serious and work harder and I know I can do this. Maybe I have learned so much now that my brain is full and will not let this in. No I can't think like that it is an excuse and I am out of them. All I can say is this is a word I do not get, I don't know where it originated from, so all I can do is keep trying. My lesson here is just to keep at it and when I learn it I will let you all know it. Let's go to number 14, it has got to be better.

14. FEELINGS: I will tell you right now that this section is very important to me. Everyone has feelings and nobody ever deserves to have their feelings hurt by others. I will never understand why anyone would want to hurt someone else, but it happens all the time. I have learned to think first and make sure that I respect the fact that people's feelings can be hurt very quickly and can end up having a   very serious outcome. I learned this because my feelings were hurt so much by everyone and they did not even know they were doing it. I know they never did this on purpose, but it was still real. I have also learned to take care of my own feelings and make sure that I am strong enough to never let anyone hurt them again. I have mentioned the phrase "false hope" before, and believe me this is something that I will never give someone. There

is absolutely no reason to make someone believe what is not true just to keep them around. It's always best to let someone go on with their life and find happiness with someone else than to hurt them. This has been a huge lesson to me, because I know that I have also done this in my life. I did it for selfish reasons and now I regret it sincerely, but it is too late to go back. I did not realize that I was doing this at the time, but as I look back at my life, I see clearly that I did. And the greatest lesson here is I have had to learn to let things go! Hypnosis has played a huge part in teaching me how to do this. When people hurt my feelings now I am able to sit back and just tell myself that it is not worth it to let anyone do this to me and I can let it go. I may get upset at first due to the fact that things are still new to me, but the more I practice it the better I get at it. I will tell you right now that if there is someone in my life that does not treat me the way I deserve to be treated, with honesty, respect and kindness, then I do not need them in my life. I will never treat another human being any other way again and we all deserve to be treated well. I often sit back and wonder if I did the right things while I was raising my children and the mistakes I made. I do not believe there is a parent in this world that has not made mistakes, but I do know that I did teach them to respect themselves and love themselves no matter what they ever did. I remember telling them so many times "Do not ever do anything that you will regret the next day," for this is a horrible feeling and you must live with it the rest of your life. Now the question is did they listen? The answer is no, not always. So I will just keep repeating myself and maybe one day it will sink in to both of them. I do know that raising a daughter and a son are like night and day. I know that Heather does not hurt people's feelings on purpose and Boof has never really cared who he hurt, not even his own mother and father (we are still working on him every day). I pray every night for peace and kindness for all in this world and maybe one day my prayer will come true! I know that my lesson has been learned and I will live this lesson forever!

15. FOREVER:I will never forget the words that Linda told me one night when I was very sick and they were "Cindy, sometimes people are put into our lives for a reason, but that does mean that they are put there to be in our lives to stay forever." I want to thank her now for teaching me one of the best lessons I will ever learn in my lifetime. I don't know how many people I have shared this with and it has really helped them, for we all thank you! This is something that I have thought about so much and I think I am finally beginning to understand it. I think to myself, how long is forever really? Well I do not think anyone knows the answer to this question, so I believe it is for as long as it is supposed to be. As we go through our journeys on this earth we have a plan mapped out by God, but we can change it at anytime. This is the good part, because if we choose the wrong road we can always turn around and go back another way. As we meet people along the way, I believe they do come into our lives to teach us something. We can listen or we can ignore the lesson and go on. Well I can tell you now I will always listen from now on and never ignore the lesson, this I will give to myself. I have also learned that if that person leaves my life there will be no sadness, just thanks for what they have brought to me. I may miss them, but I will go on and just remember them forever. I know this now to be true because as I have said before a very dear friend has just recently decided to leave my life and never be a part of it again. I really do not understand why he left, but that is not the question here. Maybe he was brought to me because God knew that I would need his support and kindness through the serious illness I would go through. And yes he did bring me these

116

things. Now that my recovery is progressing maybe it was time for him to move on and help the next person. There is a very big difference between sadness of losing someone and missing someone. My sadness for him is that he gave away someone that would have been there for him through anything that ever happened in his life, good or bad. My missing him is just that I miss the conversations we had, the fun we had, and the many laughs we shared. I had always thought that we would be friends forever, go to each other's special events, or to just be support systems for each other. There is so much I wanted to thank him for, but he chose to not be in this book, so I will never be able to do that. I am sorry for this because I wanted the world to know what a wonderful person he is and now you never will. So what is forever? I believe it is whatever we want it to be. Does it mean forever on this earth, or forever in eternity? I choose forever in eternity, this brings me the most peace and plenty of time to learn many more lessons!

16. HEART: When I think about my heart, I think about love, life, and the beating of keeping me alive. I also know now that my heart can hurt more than I could have ever imagined. I know that I shut my heart down and I believed that I would never open it again, because I knew that it would not ever heal, not after a break like it went through. Then something amazing happened and I learned that my heart heals over time and yes mine has. I have learned that I can open up my heart again and let myself let love in again. I know that it will be a long time before this happens, but I know that it will. I do not believe that humans are put on this earth not to share their hearts and be alone. The key word here is "share," not give it away. I also learned how big my heart is and I have room for a lot of love for many people in many different ways. But my biggest lesson is that I have learned that as long as you

keep your heart open, it can never be broken. I think this is why so many people broke my heart again during my illness, is because I had shut it down. This allowed my feelings to be hurt so badly by the people I love the most. I know now that I did not understand it then, but I sure do now. I know that I want to love again, for it the most wonderful feeling that I have ever experienced. Once I felt it I know that I want more and one day when I least expect it, it will happen to me and it will last for the rest of my life. This I do know for sure and I can't wait.

17. SOUL:If you want to find your soul, just look up into the sky at night and look at the moon. It is full of souls, for that is why it gets so big. When the moon fills up it releases the souls and anyone that has lost their soul can get a new one (but you must ask God for one). I had lost mine and yes I did find mine again, but this does not always happen. I had to learn how to find mine and I searched for a long time. It took faith, strength, and courage and a lot of hard work. All I knew was that I wanted mine back and I did anything to get it. I learned that our soul is responsible for our consciousness, thoughts, feelings and our will. Wow, this is a lot of responsibility for one soul. So I guess it is our non-physical self; therefore, it is our inner self. I know that I still want to be myself when I got well, only with many changes to myself. I want to be a better person in every way and do a lot of things differently in my life. I find these things are coming from within me and they are coming from my soul - these things will be told later.

18. WISHES:Every time I get the chance to drive to the beach after dark, I find that this one bright star is following me. It is always with me the entire way there and all the way back. I always make a wish to this star, but my wish is a secret or it will not come true. I find that I am making a lot of wishes these days about my future. I wish for wellness, I wish for peace, I wish for kindness for all mankind, I wish

for happiness, I wish for love again, I wish for safety for myself and my entire family and for all my brothers and sister on this earth, I wish for respect, I wish for honor, I wish for my children to have healthy and wonderful futures, I wish for happiness for all my friends, I wish for spring to hurry up and get here, I wish for everyone on this earth to find God and put him in their hearts. I could go on and on, because I never run out of wishes. Wishes to me are like hope. They give me the power to continue to have hope; therefore, I believe that they will come true. I am finding peace and wellness and many other things that I wish for. So I will keep wishing on a star and continue to find my happiness.

19. RISKS:In church one morning Schuyler did a great sermon on taking risks and finding adventures and this was something very new to me. I have never been a big risk taker or looked for adventures. But he really made me think when I left church that morning and I came to the conclusion that I might be missing out on a lot in life. My children are definitely risk takers and they are not scared of anything in this world. Me, well I went the safe route, so I guess I have missed out on a lot of fun and adventures. When Heather went to school in California she would always tell me come on jump on a plane and come see me. I did get on a plane one time and that was the worst experience of my life. I know I will never do that again, so I never went to see her. I regret this all the time and I always will. I have now vowed to myself that when I get to complete wellness and off of these horrible meds, I am going to start living life more and start taking risks and find adventures. No telling what I might find out there!

20. DREAM:This is a great lesson for me because I have never really had big dreams. I never believed that dreams would come true, so why have them. Well, I am here to tell you now that dreams do come true and in a big way! I can

remember times when I was really sick and could not get out of the bed, and I would dream that one day I would become well again and could do all the things again that I loved doing. Guess what, my dreams are coming true. I am now out of that bed and I can go out a little bit. I still have a long ways to go, but I will continue to dream and dream big. Yes, my dreams are huge and now I have the belief that that they will come true. Remember that dreams are different from wishes. Dreams are put into the universe and they will only come true if you stay positive and believe. I think it has a lot to do with the aura we put around us and live by. If we put good things out there, then we will get good things back. I also believe that our aura is connected to the moon. There are so many different stages in the moon and it changes the balance of the universe. That is why we must keep positive and keep it in our own universe. Yes, my dreams are huge and I will continue to dream and have hope. I have a lot of dreams out there, so you better hurry up and put some out there for yourself, or the universe will be filled up by mine!

21. MIRACLES:Have you ever seen a miracle happen? Have you ever wished for a miracle? I wished for a miracle and I got it, *it is me*! Am I worth it? You better believe I am! I am alive today and yes I am a miracle kept here on this earth by God. I know now that he was not ready for me yet in Heaven, so he kept me here. He is the only person that could have had the power to keep me alive and the power to let me love life again. I have seen two miracles in my profession as a nurse, so yes I did believe in them. The thing is I had no idea of the power of them. Now I do! My miracle of me reinforced my purpose on this earth, which is to help others. I believe that God wanted me here to tell my story, so that many people would learn how to believe as I learned. I have said before that the words to this book were given to me from God and that I am

just typing them. Well this is my task at this time given to me by God and I received it with opened arms. He gave me the strength and the courage to put myself out there for the world to know of my devastation and how I have found the healing process that he taught me. Who would ever have thought that I would be writing a book, but it had to come from somewhere. I do know that I would have never have done this on my own. I would have never found the words or been able to have the strength to tell all of my thoughts and feelings as I am doing. There is one thing that I never do is give advice unless I am asked for it. But now I am going to give you some advice and it is "Always believe in miracles, they do happen!"

Now that I have learned all of these lessons, I know that my life's work will be very different. I will be reaching for the stars and helping others in a completely different way, now I will tell you how...

CHAPTER SEVEN

My New Life's Work

I

Some chapters of this book have been very hard to write and some of them have been absolutely great to write. Well let me tell you now, this is the chapter I have been waiting to write. As you can see from this book my life was turned upside down and I have had to learn to put it back together again. Along the way I have found that there were many things in my life that I did not like about myself and I never even knew it. Now I do! I took many things for granted and always just trusted that nothing bad would ever happen to me. I think we all think like this to a point, but mine was completely real.

When I talk about my "New life's work," I mean this in every sense of the phrase. Yes, my life will be very different now and I can't wait to tell you how. If any of you out there is going through a hard time when you read this book, I hope that this chapter will bring to you the light that we do have the power to change the course we are on. It is never too late to do the things that we are truly meant to be doing, but to do them in a better way. With the help of many people that I have watched over my lifetime, I have found some to be happy, some to be sad, some to be angry, some to be selfish and some to just not care about anything at all. The only part that I want to be now is happy. This is why I am changing so many parts of my life and making myself look at myself differently (I will still be me, but a better me). I hope that by doing this my healing process will speed up and I will be able to start to live again in a complete way. *So let's start…*

II

I have begun by living my life for God first, all of mankind second, and myself third. What this means is that I will do the tasks that God sends to me first and above all else and do them in the best way that I can. I know now that since I have put God in my heart and opened it up to him he is sending me tasks. The first was this book to help others, I just hope that I have not let him down and have done a good job. He knows that I have never done anything like this before, but he gave me the job. I therefore; I believe that he trusts me to tell this story of my life (such a delicate story) so that others will learn to help others also. I can not wait for my next task (if I ever finish this one) and see what excitement it will bring to me. It is such a great feeling to know that God trusts me now and loves me also.

To take care of all of mankind means to me that I was put here to help others and do it the best way that I know how. I know that I love all people, no matter what. I have never been judgmental of anyone, never been racist of anyone and treat everyone with kindness and respect. I love all people of all cultures and I respect their differences. But now I know that this was enough to get by with, but I was never really doing the best that I could.

I look at people differently now and I love them in a different way, I believe the best way to say it is in a spiritual way. I now look at everyone as my brothers and sisters, not just other people. Sometimes when I sit at the beach and just watch people walking around or watch the surfers in the ocean, I see more smiles now on their faces. I think this means that I look for more happiness in people and wish for it for them. It gives me peace and laughter to see others laugh and know that they are having a great time. I am no longer jealous of their lives, because I know that my life will be that happy again too.

To take care of myself means just that, but in so many ways. Throughout my illness I have found that I never took the time to take care of me. I always took care of my children, my family, my friends, my patients, and everyone else, but never me. This has and will forever change, for now I will take care of myself and love myself as I do others. I have now learned to take the time to relax and smell the roses, and believe me this is huge! And yes, when I am able to go back to work and do the things I love to do, I will continue to do just that. I never realized how beautiful a rose really is or the beauty of its smell. Why? Because I never took the time! I have missed out on so much of the simple things in life, because I never took the time to notice them or enjoy them. Now when I go to a friends house for a cup of coffee, I will sit and actually enjoy it (I still get nervous being away from home, but I will get there). Now I realize that they are the greatest things in life, for they are simple.

I will always enjoy lighting a beautiful candle on my porch and enjoy the nighttime from now on, this is truly a time of peace and joy. I never knew that the world could be so quiet at night, but now I do. I always lived a life of such noise and commotion all the time, never stopping or slowing down for anything. But the saddest part was that I never knew how to love me. My new vow to myself is to love myself everyday no matter what! This has shown me the way to want to become healthier and appreciate the world around me much more than I ever did before. I now enjoy the daytime and the nighttime, and I look at them the same. This brings me a feeling of safety, I don't really know how to explain this, but I think it has a lot to do with trust.

III

When it comes to my children and my family, I do know that I will work harder to let them know that I love and appreciate them so very much. I will begin to learn ways to show them a new side of my life and try to help them more as they travel through their journeys. I know that the faith that I have found, I will share with them and encourage them to find the same peace and comfort that I have found in God. I will not only do this with my family, but with everyone that I know and will become to know. It's like I have found something that everyone in the world needs to experience and I am sure I can not get it to the world, but I must start somewhere. My parents have now joined my Church also and were recently baptized. This was a great day for our family and brought us a lot closer together. Just think what the world could be if everyone could feel this?

IV

I am also going to begin to live my life as a gift, because now I know how fast life can change and feel impossible. I believe we are all given this gift so that we are able to love one another and help each other through all times that we will all have to go through. I ask myself where does this gift come from, well it must be from our hearts. I think that God gives us this gift and shows us how to appreciate it, but we must learn this. I know that my life's work will involve appreciating this gift more so that I can live a kinder life for all that I know.

V

When it comes to my career as a nurse, I know that the way I will be a nurse is completely different that any way I have ever been before. I know that now I will truly take care of my patients and

I will take the time to also take care of their families. I know that I will never be what is considered a floor nurse again because I remember nights when I came home and did not even remember my patients names. Nursing has taken a turn for the worse in my opinion and I would love to see this change in the near future. I think that I may become a nurse in the field of Psychology, seeing as how I now know that my compassion for these patients will be stronger and I will be much more caring. I have been through this now and I think that I can understand them in a different light.

I would also like to go into teaching at some point, also in the Psychology field. I would love to speak at group sessions and to people that are going to go to work in this field. One thing I have learned is that these patients need treatment that is completely different than any other patients. It would be great to speak at training sessions for new employees, for I truly want them to understand this. I have been in every field of nursing and I do know now that this field is very different. It takes a very special kind of person to work in this field and I believe that I can be one of them.

I know that it is easy to say that we all learned about depression, panic and anxiety in nursing school, and yes I thought back then that it must be a terrible thing to go through. I do not remember ever learning about what can happen to a person that goes into a complete shock over a tragic event and what it can do to them. Now that I do, I plan to let the world know about it and how to treat people going through this. My philosophy is that an addict knows recovery, an alcoholic knows recovery, and a cardiac patient knows heart problems, now I know shock. I believe that people that have gone through these problems are the best to teach others, for they can share what no books can teach you.

I can actually see myself sitting in the same room at the mental hospital I was in and talking to the people that are sitting in the same chairs that I have sat in so many times. This is where I feel that I am needed the most. I know their tears, their fears, their loneliness and their loss of hope to live. I know that they feel sick from all the new meds and how they want to only stay in their room and be alone. It is so hard sometimes to sit in groups and try to listen and understand when you are so nauseated, dizzy, and panicked. It is the most horrible feeling in the world and one that I do not think that I could ever live through again. This is why it is so important to heal correctly the first time! I have talked about how long the healing process takes and this is really important for these patients to understand. I do not know at this time when I will be back at work or even going to a restaurant with music playing, but I know now that I will. In this way I can give them hope, and this will possibly begin their healing process. If it takes the rest of my life, I know that I will have my voice heard, and it will be heard by as many people as I can possibly get to. I will start at the bottom and work my way up to the top, but I will get there!

VI

One of the biggest parts of my new life's work is going to be to take the time to listen to others (especially my family and friends) and taking their advice, this I will do for me. I have a lot of work to do on myself and I think that I need to start here. I have always been good at giving advice, but never good at taking it. I don't want to think that I thought I knew it all, but maybe I did when it came to me. Marie tells me that I always lived life in a very non-chalant way and nothing ever bothered me. She told me just the other night that when I was married to Billy, everyone thought we were so happy. Then one morning I walked into her house and said "Well Billy is moving out today and we are getting a divorce." She says I said it like it was just another thing in my life and just another day. I just went on and continued life as normal and it was no big deal to me. When I think of this I find that it is very true and I never realized it. I knew that Billy would be in our lives forever as my children's father, so it wasn't like he was gone, he just didn't live there anymore. Boy do I think of things differently now. I am looking for answers from my family and friends to help me with my past and trying to figure out where the problems were and when they began. I know that I will be bringing up a lot of my past, but I know that I will learn a lot about myself that will help me a lot for my future.

My new vow to me (another one) is to listen to others and truly understand what I can learn from them. I know that there are a lot of things in my past that I have to let go of and I know that this is going to be a hard process, but I have to do it for wellness. Through a lot of therapy I have come to the conclusion that there were a lot of things leading up to my illness and X just put the icing on the cake. This may not be true at all, but I must find out. So I am going back and looking at myself and I will work on my previous problems and try my best to solve them, for this is not going to be easy but very necessary. I find myself trying to only think of tomorrow and forgetting about yesterday, but this is not a part of true healing. All I know is now I have to learn patience, so I sure hope everyone is ready, for they are definitely going to have to help me.

VII

As I look back to what I have written in this chapter, I look at it as an adventure with plenty of risks. I only hope that my recovery will continue and I will be able to do all the things for other as I wish to do. I know that there will be plenty of hard times ahead to do the things I want to do, but what is life without risks? I believe that these risks are well worth taking and I am not ever going to stop.

I realize now that in my career as a nurse that money was very important to me, but what did I really gain from it? The answer is not a lot of happiness and not a lot of feelings of doing the best job that I could have done. I have now learned to live a very simple life, and no I can not go and buy anything I want, but you know what, I am finding more laughter and more self-worth. I will never compromise my patients in the ways that I did before, because I know that we will all be there in that bed one day. I want a nurse like the nurse that I am going to be when I am able. I will advocate for my patients and I will use my voice more when I see where changes need to be made. *This you can count on…*

CHAPTER EIGHT

My Blessings
(In Disguise)

As I have written this book, I have realized that my blessings are the people that have been with me throughout this whole ordeal. I have decided to end the book in a very personal way, with letters. I am going to write a letter to everyone and anyone that wants to write a letter to me can. I have made a rule for the letters, the rule is nobody can read each others letters until they all are written and ready to go. That way there is no play on each others letters in any way.

There is one thing that I want you all to know and that is how important communication is for a person as sick as I was. I am talking about communication between my doctors, my pharmacist, and my family. My mom was the one who carted me off to all of my doctors appointments and got to know them all. She put all of her faith in them as much as I did. I had Fred talking to Karen, then Fred talking to Dr. Z., and all of them with my family. I hope that these letters will show this in every way.

These letters are from my heart and soul and are being written with all of the love that I have to give to each and every one of you. For everyone has played such an incredible part in my life in the last year and a half, for that I do not know how to ever thank them enough, so now I am going to try.

There have been a lot of parts in this book where I have cried my eyes out and believe me this is going to be a chapter of tears. I am just thankful now that the tears are "happy tears." I can not wait to get all of your letters, because I know our letters will be so much alike (even though we did not read each others). *So this final chapter is for everyone I love so much*!

My Dearest God:

As I sit here tonight and write this letter to you, I wonder as I always do as to what I will say when I finally get to meet you. I know that I will thank you for giving me this beautiful earth that I have lived on for so long, for my beautiful children and family you have blessed me with, my wonderful friends you have given me, and most of all for loving me and being in my heart. I know that I will thank you for coming to me in my worst times of need, and yes you always have. I know I will thank you for welcoming me into Heaven and wrapping me in your strong arms and allowing me to spend eternity with you.

I also want to thank you for taking care of all of my loved ones that have been there with you before me. I know that when I see them again, they will have smiles on their faces and will be happy. I know that you give them the power to watch over me and make sure that I am ok.

I know that I will thank you for the ocean, the moon, the sun and the stars that I have loved all of my life. The power that you have given us in the ocean for healing is phenomenal. You have given us the moon to hold our souls and give us new ones, the sun for warmth, and the stars to show us the way. I will thank you for the nature that is all around us, wow just to listen to the birds sing is so peaceful. I know they talk to me and send me messages from you.

I also will thank you for my ability to find strength and courage when I needed it the most and the ability to find my power again. I understand now why you gave me the tools and made me do the work, for I would have never learned the lessons that I did if you would have done it for me. Now I know that I will always be able to use my tools when I need them because I learned this. This is what taught me to never doubt your plan for me in any way ever again.

Thank you for walking by me when I can walk and carrying me when I can not. Thank you for watching over my children as they grow and learn as we all have to do. Thank you for accepting them into your hands when I could no longer care for them, I knew they would be safe with you.

Last but not least, thank you for me!

Every ounce of my love, Cindy

Dear Pastor Schuyler:

This is a letter that is proof positive of how God works in such mysterious ways. God sent me to many great people for my recovery and then he sent me to you and your Church Family. I have written how I became to know you and your sermons help me everyday of my life. I know that I can always hear your voice at any time by just turning on my computer. I want you to know how much peace and comfort this brings to me. I thank you very much for putting your sermons online for all of us to hear at anytime.

I also would like to thank you for taking time with me and talking to me about my illness and answering questions that I was unsure of. Your compassion and caring was felt very strongly by me, this is when I knew I would be a part of your family. I also have mentioned that it is very rare to meet people that are doing what they were born to do, this is exactly what you are doing. I know that this illness has changed my life forever and I will live my life differently now, which includes helping people in many different ways, having forgiveness in my heart and most importantly living my life for God.

It gives me great comfort knowing that you and the other pastors at your church will always be there for me at anytime I need them (and how wonderful they are), and this I truly know in my heart to be true. I pray every night that everyone in this world can become as lucky as I have become in finding my House of God, for it sure does make your life wonderful. Every morning of my life now as I thank God for giving me another day with my family, I also count down the days until Sunday will be here again and I can come to my God's House. It is like walking on a cloud!

Thank you for accepting me into your Church and giving me all that you have. I know I have found my home and it all came about by your sermons of fear, I know in my heart you were preaching to me and you didn't even know it. God's plan is truly incredible, for when I threw out another lifeline you were there to catch it and yes you did hold on tight!

God Bless you and yours, Cindy

My Dearest Daughter Heather:

Hi Honey, you know the greatest thing about being a mom? The greatest thing is that I can tell you what to do for the rest of your life. But, the problem with you is that you have never allowed anyone to tell you how to do anything, it was always your way or no way! This is your greatest asset my love.

I apologize so much for getting so sick and having to leave your life for so long. But I want to thank you for all that you were able to do for me, with work and Ben and all, I know that you did your very best. I hope I did not scare you, but I think this illness did. All I know is that I missed you so much, but now you are back home and with me anytime I need you.

Now I am going to give you some advice and I hope you listen this time, for this is the best advice you will ever get in your life! You must always love God first and if he is not in your heart yet, call for him and ask him to keep you and watch over you, for this will make you life the best it could ever be. Then I want you to love yourself no matter what you do. Remember that you have a purpose on this earth and you do have a right to be here. Then I want you to never give your power away to anyone, this does not mean to not love, just keep your power. Always keep your family first, for they are the ones that will never leave you no matter what, everyone else can and will. Hold your friends dear and always be there for them, for you will need them one day. But most of all never forget that you have a voice and I want you to use it! Last but not least never forget "Mama knows best!"

These lessons were very hard for me to learn that is why I am teaching them to you now. This way you will never have to go through the pain that I have had to endure and you will always be safe. I know in my heart that you will always be safe now and that is all I need to love life again and go on.

When I asked God for you, I had no idea he would give me the best daughter in the world, boy did I get lucky! I will always be here for you no matter what and will never leave you again, this I promise!

All my love, mom

Dear Mom,

I suppose the first thing that I want to say to you is thank you. Thank you for being my mom, my friend, and my teacher. I don't know if I have ever said that to you enough, I don't know if anyone has ever said that to their mother enough. I am one of the luckiest people that I know for having someone like you there to support me throughout the years.

I know that the last year and a half has been a rough one for you, much more so than for any of the rest of us. I will admit that it was not easy to watch someone you love and respect go to a place that renders them almost unrecognizable, but in the end we all made it, and I think we all ended up better people for it.

I remember when it all began, it was just after my last knee surgery. You called out of work to take care of me, and to this day you have not been back. All however, is okay for the journey that we have all taken with you has been more inspiring and more educational than any other path we could have walked down. In the beginning I think we all were at a loss for what to do about your situation. It was something that no one in the family had ever seen or dealt with first hand. I know that I was going through a whole spectrum of feelings, many very selfish. I had always known my mom to be the lady with the answers, the optimism, the sarcastic wit, and the strength to help me get out of whatever delima I could get myself into. Now seeing this person who I didn't know crying all the time, feeling sorry for herself, and many times not even able to conjure the strength to get out of bed, was so alien to me that I found myself avoiding the situation entirely. It broke my heart to see you like that, and after a while I found myself without the strength to face it. For that, I am forever sorry. I should have been there. Many times I would think to myself, what would my mother say to me if she found me lying in bed crying over things that were done and over... she would tell me to "quit my crying, get out of the damn bed, and go make a new opportunity for myself". So I tried that, I yelled at you to get over all the sadness and give me my mom back. The look in your eyes that day absolutely killed me, and I knew then that we were all dealing with something much more serious than any of us had imagined. When you went to the hospital just days later, I sat with Mema and Papa in the waiting room, each of us looking defeated, and we realized that in order to bring you back we were going to have to drive down a long winding bumpy road... We vowed to take turns in the driver seat, and travel all night long if that was what it took, anything as long as we got you back home to us in one piece.

Slowly, slowly, day by day another step was taken. Some forwards, some backwards, finding the right doctors, finding the right medicines, finding the right words to inspire you each day to just hold on and it would get better. And in the end, often after arguing and wanting to give up, you found that one last ounce of strength that God had allotted for you on that given day, and you used it to make it to the next one. It was all we could hope for, and every day we were so proud of you. You would muster up a smile and go to sleep in hopes that the next day would be the breakthrough.

Then, finally after months of hard work, exhaustion, and patience.... a breakthrough. You called me giggling, seems simple enough, but for all of us it was the first time you had truly smiled in almost a year and more importantly, you really meant it. You were laughing... I can only speak for myself when I say that I didn't know if it was real. It was only the day before when you were wondering if you would have the strength to wake up the next morning, and here you were laughing your ass off on the phone with me. I had to call Meme and Papa to see if they were seeing it too. They were... overnight you came out of it, you were really coming back to us. After all of this time watching you slip seemingly ever deeper into an abyss that I could not be sure you would find your way out of, you... and only you, found the patience, the strength, and the sheer will to make through, what I now know to be, one of the most difficult and exhausting illnesses in existence. You made it and I am so proud of you. One of the most impressive parts of the whole ordeal to me is that, through it all you remained true to form... as the teacher. Everyone around you has learned a valuable lesson about life through your recent experience. Mema and Papa learned how to be the caregiver in the truest sense of the word, Boofey learned not to take for granted the people who he loves and who love him, Aunt Sharon learned that we all do need her very much and that she is one of the rocks of the family and she should be proud of herself, Aunt Marie found closure in one of her best friends that she had missed for a few tragic years, and then there is me. I think this taught me many lessons, the

most important being a deeper understanding of the word compassion than I had ever fathomed to exist. Learning that it is not always how you are looking at a situation, but seeing something truely through the eyes of someone else. Learning that sometime a sickness really is in someones head, which makes it a hell of alot more difficult to work through, but not impossible. Learning that faith sometimes is the most reliable and powerful medecine.
You taught us all that, even while lying in bed crying, you really are a powerful lady. If you ever feel like you are forgetting the power that you have over all of us, I want you to remember that. Mom, I love you more than I could ever make clear using just words and this piece of paper, I am emensly proud of you and grateful for what you have done for the rest of us. I know it was probably the craziest road that could have been traveled to get us all to where we are now, but here we all are, at the end... smiling.
I love you, never stop smiling, you deserve all the happiness that this world has to offer.
Your little girl,
Heather

My Dearest Son Boof:

Well when you read this book I know you are going to be furious because I called you Boof, but oh well you are my little boy Boof and always will be, so get over it! Hi my wonderful son, yes I do love you and I always will no matter what you could ever do or what you have done in the past. Yes, you do know how to break my heart, but I am glad those days are over now. I also know that when I asked God for the perfect son, I got him!

I am also sorry for leaving you too for so long during my illness. I know that you had no idea what to do for me and that is ok. You were not supposed to understand all of that, but what gives me peace is that you tried and that is all I needed. But I must say "Wet Willies" would never have been the answer, sorry! But I am coming back now and wow I see so many changes in you now. Wow what a few years can do. You are truly growing up now and I can see it and it sure does look good.

Now I get to tell you also that I get to tell you what to do all of your life just because I am your mom. Now I get to give you advice, and I want   you to find God also if you have not already and bring him to your heart. Then I want you to learn respect for yourself and everyone else, for everyone deserves it especially you for yourself. This will make you a much happier person inside which will make you life better on the outside. Then I want you to love yourself and begin to think about your future in a better way. You have the power to become anything you want to be and you have the intelligence to do it. Next I want you to learn honesty and be honest to yourself and others. I think this is something that is coming to you now, for this I can also see.

Please take these lessons and make your life easier and happier. Let God guide you and follow his path, he will lead you to happiness. Remember that I will always be here now for anything that you ever need and I want to thank you for teaching me forgiveness. This has made my life much easier and happier.

Never forget that "Mama knows best," for I also told your sister this, so get it and never forget it!

I love you, mom

My Beloved Mom:

I remember other times that I have written you letters and I am glad this is a different situation (I was in jail last time). I am sure glad that those days are over, but then it was your turn to scare me to death. You became so very sick and I am so sorry that I did not know what to do for you. When I think of all you did for me when I was sick for the first 14 years of life and I had no clue what to do for you. I guess that is the difference between a mom and a son. All I know is that you were so sad and cried all the time. I wanted to just pick you up and get you well, but it didn't work that way. I did not think a person could cry so much.

I told you one time that you were "The Queen of my Heart" and yes you are and always will be. You have been there for me no matter what I ever put you through and always loved me anyway. How lucky are Header and I to have a mom like that.

It is so cool to see you laugh again and be able to sit outside with us on the carport. As we talk about things now, I think I understand them better, but I still ask myself "why you?" You always took care of everything and did everything for everybody. Then all of a sudden it was like bam you were gone. You tell me now that you still have a long ways to go, but that's ok now because at least you laugh and are not in the bed.

I know you can still not go out to many places yet, but "Wet Willies" is waiting for us when you are ready (ha ha). I would just be happy to take you to dinner or a movie one night (I will even pay), just let me know when you are ready and if we have to leave that's ok too.

I love you more than life itself mom and I know we are both going to be ok. It's so cool you wrote a book and yes I am going to read it. Thanks for typing this letter for me, you type a lot faster than me. I loved writing it!

Your little boy, Boof

143

Dear Mom and Dad:

The very first sentence of my book says that I was born to the two coolest parents in the world, well now I know that I was born to the two greatest parents on the face of the earth. I am going to try my best to get through this letter, it will be very hard!

I want to apologize from my whole heart for what I put you through. I know it was horrible for you both, I only hope that you understand that I did not know at the time what I was doing. As long as I have been a nurse, I never knew that anyone could ever be as sick as I was. And the two of you had to see it first hand, your own baby daughter.

There is one point I want to stress so much is that you both did an incredible job in a situation you have never been in before. You both gave up your lives to take care of me for a very long time, when I could not do anything for myself. This I do not ever know how to thank you for. I remember times when I would tell you things, for example: I can not get in the shower without you (mom) sitting in there with me, or that I can not watch TV or read without getting dizzy. I know that you did not understand these things, but believe me they were real. I know that you understand this now.

If there is anything good that came out of this, it is that I now know that I never have to worry about anything in my life, because I have you two. I think I always knew this, but now I really do know it. I felt so guilty for everything, especially not being able to pay my bills or buy my own food. But you always told to forget that, you would do anything it took so that we would all have what we needed, and that is exactly what you did!

So I am thanking you both again for everything you did for me and for teaching me that this really is a true family in all meanings of the word. Now if you can only teach me how to keep a husband, then you would have done something!

Every ounce of my love, Cindy

Dear Cindy

This letter will not be what you think. I believe there is a higher power that makes us what + who we are and that can change in the blink of an eye. The last year has proven this with you. It was a good thing that me + Pa Pa had a phone with 911 on it and a new truck to follow you to every ER in the Chas. area. I learned Patience in all the waiting rooms. If anyone ever looked in my wallet they would think I am as crazy as a loon with all the business cards I have from all your Drs + hospitals. It is by the Grace of God and Family that we are all recovering slowly but surely. As Scarlett would say "tomorrow is another day", for us to sit out and drink coffee + have a cigarette and give Pa Pa a hard time.

All My Love to
you My Baby Girl

Mom

Cindy,

You know your dad has really had a hard time understanding what really happen to you, but it was really a bad time in our home for about a year and a half, but now you have made a great come back.

People who have never had this happen to them or a love one just don't know how bad it really is, you lay in your bed at night just knowing you are going to hear your daughter hollow for you, thank god those days are gone.

"Thank God we have our Daughter back"

Love Always
Dad

146

My Dearest Sister, Sharon:

When I sit down to write your letter, I do not even know where to begin. After all the things we have been through together the last two years, makes me wonder why we were never this close all our lives. All I can say now is, I am so glad we have found our way to each other.

I want to thank you for all that you have done for me to keep me alive during this terrible illness. You were always there for me at anytime day or night and this I will never forget. I remember the times you came and stayed with me, held onto me and cried with me. Your compassion and love gave me the hope to go on and try harder for wellness.

Believe me I know what a pain in the ass I was to you, calling you ten times a day and driving you completely crazy, and all the time you were also taking care of Nana. I don't know how you did it, but you always made the time for both of us, that's pretty incredible! You sat with both of us at the hospital many times and you never complained for a minute. That's a true loving person.

Then when it was time for me to start going out a little bit, you took me to Barry's and always watched out for me. You must have asked me a million times if I was ok and this was in a 30 minute period. I think this was when I began to laugh a little bit, yes you'll are quite a crew. So I am ending you and Barry's letters the same and I hope it brings back great memories for both of you. Thank you again for all and I will never let you go again. Sing with me and smile!

Whenever I wake-up
Before I put on my make-up,
I say a little prayer for you!
I'm combing my hair now
Wondering what dress to wear now,
I say a little prayer for you!
Forever and ever
You'll stay in my heart
And I will love you

There will never be
Heartbreak for you!

Remember this song forever and never forget those times of therapy and love, for I never will.

I love you forever, Cindy

To My Dearest Sister, Cindy

I really don't know how, or where to start. In the past, my sister and I were never really that close. We often disagreed on things and are very different. I hate to say it but her getting sick has brought us closer than any sister could ask for. Don't get me wrong we still disagree about things but that's OK. I feel she knows now that I will always be there for her. I now love her dearly and am so glad she is feeling better. I have a best friend in my life whom is very close to me, but a sister is something different. Unfortunately, Cindy lost her best friend tragically many years ago. I'm sure she still thinks about her. Over the past 2 yrs I have become a caregiver to two very different people in my life. All of a sudden (BAM) after spending lots of time with both of these very strong willed women

I came to love them both dearly. Unfortunately I lost one of these women (my Mother-in-Law) to cancer and my sister is recovering quite well. Now I know how to appreciate every single minute of every single day of my life. So now I'm going to end this letter with the fact that I have been blessed to have my Sister back in my life and will never let go of her again.

Love Ya!

Sharon

My Dearest Brother Lance:

You know what I got the greatest parents, the greatest siblings, and the greatest children, and the greatest friends, how lucky am I? Yes, I did get the greatest brother and I am so glad. It is so cool and this whole family has come back together at this time. I know that you were so busy with your restaurant when I was so sick, and you probably did not understand any of it either. You guys, none of you got it! That's ok, I think you see it now and it is great to be seeing you all the time now.

I thought of you all the time and missed you a lot. I think I put you in shock on Christmas Day in 2007 when you saw me in the bed so sick for the first time. I am sorry for that, but I am kind of glad I don't remember a lot of it. But I remember that hug you gave me and telling me "It is all going to be ok!" These are the things I do remember and will never forget. The one thing I did know was that if I needed you, you would have been there and this was priceless.

You, Sharon and I have missed so much time together in our lives and it is so great now that we all see each other so much now. You see, this illness was a blessing in so many ways.

I just want you to thank yourself everyday for being a great brother and a very special part of this family. We have been talking a lot lately about how lucky we are to have the family we have, because now you are sick and waiting for surgery at this time. Do not worry I will be there for you in any way I can. I love you to death and thanks for all.

All my love, Little sister Cindy

Dear Cindy,

I Love you with all of my heart and feel honored that you request that I write a letter for this book.

I, like so many others, know that you have been through a horrible, dark, terrible time in your life with this illness that you have. I only wish that I had known how to help you, but nobody did.

I do know that yourself, our sister Sharon, and myself are definitely the most blessed children on this planet. We have the most wonderful parents, we believe in God from the bottom of our hearts, and we are a pure, close, very strong family.

Cindy, I know that you have spent a lot of time and energy to write this book solely to explain what you went through and help others to understand this illness. I will continue to pray that it does just that.

P.S. Our belief in God and our family will get us through anything!

With All My Love,
Big Brother
Lance

Dear Lucy (my cat),

I have to tell you all that my little Lucy was by my side 24 hours a day when I was so sick, I know she felt my pain. She would lie beside me or sit on top of me all the time.

When I was crying all the time, she came up and put her face on mine one night and licked my tears away, yes she knew.

How lucky am I, I even have the greatest pet on the planet and she could never have been left out of this book. I tell her all the time she better not ever leave me for there will never be another like her.

So thank you Lucy, my Lucy Bell for all your love and support!

All my love, mom

My Dearest Fred:

I don't even know how to start to thank you for everything you have done for me during the worst time in my life. I thank God everyday for bringing you back into my life in such a sad way, but such a God like way. How God knows to do the things he does just amazes me. When I dumped myself on your doorstep, you just took me in and gave me such hope and tried your best to make me feel better. I hardly remember so much of those times, but I do remember you compassion and kindness.

I want to apologize for driving you absolutely crazy, for I know I did. I called you everyday and sometimes more than once. I called you in the middle of the night so many times, but you always took the time for me and talked to me and made me feel better. When I look back at my journals now and I see how much I bothered you, I just want to say I am so sorry. I do know that you will probably never give your cell phone number out again!

I know I don't see you anymore, but I sure do miss you and Francis so much. She was such a trooper too and always helped so much when you were busy with someone else. I also want to thank you for sending me to Karen which has been one of the best things I have ever done in my life. I use Hypnosis everyday in my life, what a gift she has given me. Then you send me to Dr. Z. to carry me through the rest of my recovery, these people are truly blessings in my life.

If there ever comes a day when you or your family ever needs a nurse, you know you can always call on me and I will be there in a flash. I don't have much more to offer, but I am a great caregiver.

So thank you for all, I miss you all, and you will forever be in my heart for all you did for me. You saved my life so many times and this I will carry with me forever. There are not many like you in this world and I thank God everyday of my life for you.

God Bless you and yours, Cindy

Dear Dr. Zealberg:

Hi Dr. Z., it's me you know the one who has been the test of your career. Believe me a lot of Doctor's can say that right now. I just want to let you know how wonderful you have been to me by taking me into your care as quickly as you did. I thank God everyday for leading me to Fred so that he could lead me to you.

I mentioned in my book that it is not very often that you find a Doctor that just fits with your needs, but I sure got lucky. I have felt so safe since being in your care and believe me that has been huge in my recovery process. The fact that I can reach you at anytime is very peaceful and calming and I believe that is why I have not had to call you often, it's just knowing you are there. I know that Fred brought me as far as he could and he knew just where to send me to finish my healing process.

I want to thank you for just being the Doctor you are, your encouragement and kindness has made me believe that I will get completely well one day. I was so sick when I started with you and look at me now. I know I have a long ways to go to get rid of the fears and panic, but we are doing it!

Oh and by the way, even when I do get well, I am not going to stop being your patient, I like the feeling of walking on clouds when I leave your office and I am never going to let that end. I don't really want to say "Just get used to it," but what I am trying to say is, "Just get used to it!"

So thank yourself everyday for making such a huge difference in so many people's lives, for you truly do.

God Bless you and yours, Cindy

Dear Karen:

The first thing I want to say is thanks Fred for sending me to you. What a gift I ended up getting, a gift that I will take with me and use for the rest of my life. Hypnosis has ended up being one of the best things I have ever done for myself, who would have ever thought? All I have to do now is think your name and I start to relax and hear your voice.

I want to thank you for all of your compassion and hope that you continuously gave me. I have mentioned that I hardly remember those times because I was so sick, but it sure sunk in. You were always there for me anytime I needed you and this is what I want you to thank yourself for everyday. You were a huge part in saving someone's life, what a gift God has given you.

I encourage people all the time now to do hypnosis for so many reasons, because they see what it has done for me. I do not usually give out advice, but this advice I do give. Thank you again and get ready, because when I get ready to quit smoking, you know where I will come.

God Bless you and yours, Cindy

628 St. Andrews Blvd., Charleston, SC 29407
(843) 225 – 3036

Dear Cindy,

When you came to me as a client on Dr. Fred Pooser's referral we laid out a plan of action. Included in that plan were the following: Elimination of panic attacks, reduce depression, increase self confidence, eliminate anxiety, learning to relax, improvement of concentration, anger management, eliminate guilt, reduce frustration, forget the person who you felt ignited your depression, and develop a positive attitude, - plateful at best. I gave us 14 weeks to accomplish these behavioral and attitudinal changes.

To address these changes I did the first couple of sessions specifically dealing with: eliminating panic attacks, anxiety, creating a positive attitude, encouraging a sense of self control, empowerment and stress reduction. We moved on understanding that there was a "Wind of Change" afoot and we did several sessions on letting go of the past and releasing problems and changing that negative thinking that no longer served you and past memories in general including those of X. We focused on surviving a breakup and removing someone from your mind along with several sessions dedicated to developing courage, self confidence, building self esteem and self worth and general emotional healing. We worked with developing positive self talk and techniques to learn to reject negative thoughts and to learn acceptance. We spent two sessions concentrating on removing withdrawal symptoms from your numerous medications. We finished out the program with work on self discipline, becoming success conscious and enjoying life.

When you first came in Cindy, you were in tears, shaky and very thin. There was an air of helplessness and hopelessness about you. You were totally preoccupied with your medications. You felt your life hung in the balance because of your medications (this preoccupation may have come from your nursing background.) At first most feedback from you was about your medications and you did not seem inclined to listen to your tapes. But slowly you began to do so more and more. Dr. Pooser and I also communicated about your situation and agreed you needed a new psychiatrist as the one you had seemed unavailable most of the time and just recommended increasing doses. Dr. Pooser found a jewel in Dr. Zealberg. He was just what you needed and he began to remove you from some of the medications and gradually wean you off the one giving the most trouble. From your reports he was supportive and kind.

The transition to who you are today from who you were when you first came into my office was slow but sure. Gradually you began to look better and you even began to laugh, such a good sign. As a clinician, when we hear that first laugh from a client, we know we are "half way home."

And the most wonderful part of hypnosis is that I can't do anything to you I just help you to access your own resources. To think you had all those resources just waiting to be used when you felt you had none. They just needed to be awakened.

Today you are a joyful person Cindy, with a bright future before you. You have yourself back which is wonderful for you and for us who did not know that "you."

Your book can be a real help to others going through a dark emotional tunnel. It lets them understand there is indeed a light at the end of that tunnel. You also give caretakers clear ideas of "what to do." It is very often puzzling to the caretakers, friends and families of a person taking this dark and devastating journey how best to help. This is a good handbook.

Take care and live and love your life thoroughly. The world is waiting for your full comeback.

Sincerely,

Karen (Hoad) CHT

My Dearest Rosie:

Do you believe I have known you for 33 years now, Wow, that's pretty cool? I met you when I was only 17 years old when we started working together. My first job, that left me with a dear friend for life. Now how many people can say that? The bad part is, I think we are getting old (ha ha).

I know that I did not let you know that I was sick, because I did not want you to worry about me and I knew you would have. But now that my recovery is progressing it has been great to see you again and hear you kind and heart felt words of encouragement. I could write this letter forever and never be able to tell you how much I love you and appreciate your friendship. I often wonder what our boss in Heaven thinks of us as he watches over us. I know he thinks it is amazing how we have stayed so close and I love this. We have probably made him turn over in his grave a few times, but I am sure he was laughing when he did.

I want to thank you for being with me now and you know that I will never let you go. You will forever be in my heart and I will always be there for you no matter what, just holler!

I love you, Cindy

Cindy Leopard

MAIL
Classic

Overdue letter you asked for

From: "Rosiebud31@aol.com" <Rosiebud31@aol.com>

To: leopard_cindy@yahoo.com

Dear Cindy,

Your idea of writing a book about your experiences is a wonderful, generous one. There are so many people in this world who are hurting mentally, to one degree or another, who need encouragement and hope that they can find the way and means to stop the hurting. When you were ready to cope with seeing even old friends for the first time, it was heart-wrenching to see what a mental illness can do to a person, and it was hard to even imagine what you must have gone through and what still lay ahead for a good recovery. I'm glad you found your strength in a loving God and family and friends and that the right course of treatment was provided for you. If even one person can benefit from this book, the effort you've put into writing it will have been priceless. We're all looking forward to a bright future for you and are happy to have our "old Cindy" back with a lot of the "new Cindy" mixed in.

With love,

Rosie

160

My best friend forever, Marie:

Wow, to think of the things we have done in the last 28 years is awesome. We have truly been through the best of times and the worst of times. But we always made it, no matter what! These have been the best years of my life. You quickly became my children's second mother, their God mother and I always knew that if anything ever happened to me you would always keep them in your life. Thank you for that!

I want you to know what a huge part of my recovery you were and you did not even realize it. I also never let you know how truly sick I was, I don't know why, I guess I just wasn't thinking. But there was one thing you did for me that I will forever be grateful for. You gave me so much strength and courage as I would lie there at night in the days when all I wanted to do was die. I would lie there and think of how strong you were and how much courage you had when you went through something a million times worse than I could ever imagine. It gave me hope that if you could get through those horrible times, I had to be able to get through this. So even though you were not actually there with me, believe me you were there in so many ways. I talked to you everyday and believe me I could hear your voice talking back to me. I think you were saying something like this "Girl, screw that guy, he isn't worth it, he is a jerk, get up and move on." Does that sound about right?

And then when I started to feel a little better, I knew where my second home was and I came to you. I was so scared I was going to upset you and bring back memories for you, but you assured me it was ok. I feel like it kind of broke the ice and we both started talking and helping each other a lot. This I thank you for with all my heart.

All I can say is I love you and your family to death, your children are like my own, and now I feel like I have some grandbabies because I have yours. So just hang in there with me, put the coffee on when I call and get over me driving you crazy now. When I need to get out, I just go to whoever will let me in their house and I end up at yours a lot. Thanks for never kicking me out and always being there for me.

All my love forever, Cindy

From: jmizzell@aol.com
To: leopard_cindy@yahoo.com
Subject: Letter for book
Date: Wed, 18 Mar 2009 6:51 pm

March 18, 2009

Hi Cindy,

Don't faint & fall over dead - I know you have been waiting a long time for this letter and I do apologize for taking so long but I'm just not a writer. It takes me a long time to gather up all of my thoughts and commit them to paper. Anyway, here goes.

We have been dear friends for many years. I remember when Billy brought you to our house to meet us for the first time. I think it was about 30 years ago - darn you're getting old. We were in such shock because we didn't even know Billy was seeing anyone steady - much less thinking about getting married but that's our girl Cindy - ready to get it done - whirlwind romance. Then a few years later came the best of both of you. Heather (my Goddaughter) and Benjamin (Boofer). We had some good times hanging out with each other and all of the children. My sister in law Bonnie and her two children - me & my three & you and your two.
My kids thought going over to your house for TV dinners was the greatest - they loved it and your kids thought coming over to my house for a home cooked meal was the greatest. I tried to teach you how to cook but you were unteachable (I know why).

After the breakup of you and Billy and the divorce (another shocker) then came Steve. Always keeping us guessing - never know which way you're going. You were in Nursing school while you dated (and married) Steve and after what seemed like an eternity you graduated and became the wonderful nurse we all knew you would be. We hung out more when you and Steve dated than when the two of you were married. You and Steve moved West Ashley and we stayed in the same place so we didn't see too much of each other for awhile.

When you and Steve broke up and went your seperate ways I began to see you a little more. We would go out to lunch to "BoBo's" just before you had to go off to work. Then I didn't see you so much again because you had found the love of your life. I didn't know him or anything about him except what you told me a few times. I was very sorry to hear about the breakup of your relationship and even more sorry to know that you were so devastated. I did not know the extent of your emotional breakdown at the time. I would have been there for you if I had known. Sometimes you have to do things your own way and I do not fault you for keeping things to yourself.

I am just so glad that you are back to your old self and doing so much better. You know I love you girl and will always be here for you if you need me. God does not give us more than we can handle. There is a lesson in this even if we can't see it yet.

Love,
Marie

Dear Sam:

Hey girl: How are things in Virginia? I was sitting here trying to think of how many years I have known you and I think it's about 12 now. Wow the things we have been through, remember Nursing School; do you feel the panic? I do! You do know that I never would have gotten through that without you and your brains. As much work and time you put in with me on the cardiac system, you would have thought I could have at least passed the test, but no I flunked it, and boy did I flunk it (I guess nobody will ever hire me again as a cardiac nurse now). I apologize for that, you tried so hard.

I apologized in my book for hurting your feelings so badly when I did not come to Virginia, but now I want to thank you for your forgiveness. I promise I never meant to hurt you, for I would never do that, but the point is I did. I do know that I never will again!

Thank you for always being with me throughout my terrible illness, even though you were not here, you were in my heart. I must have called and cried to you a million times, but you were always there for me. Of course you are another friend I am so glad that I have in my life. I just miss you so much not being in Charleston anymore and I wish all the time that you would come home.

It was so cool seeing you last month for the first time in three years, and even going out to dinner. I will never forget you telling me "Oh shut up, if you have a panic attack just go outside and have it and come back when it's over, I'm hungry!" Well you scared that panic attack right out of me, and I actually did well. It was my first time in a restaurant in almost two years, yeah! It was so good to see you and I hated it when you left to go back. Please come back soon, until then I will come there whenever I am able.

I just want you to appreciate yourself for being such a true friend and helping me so much, and if you ever need anyone you know I will always be there by phone or in person. I appreciate

KD for introducing us and nursing school for bringing us back together. I love you to death and always will.

God Bless you, Cindy Lou Hoo

--- On **Thu, 3/19/09, samshannonrn@aim.com <*samshannonrn@aim.com*>** wrote:

From: samshannonrn@aim.com <samshannonrn@aim.com>
Subject: Letter
To: leopard_cindy@yahoo.com
Date: Thursday, March 19, 2009, 9:03 PM

To My Life Long Friend, Cindy.

Individuals cross our path everyday, but once in a while a force not very well understood bonds two people and a

friendship begins. For many, the word friendship is nothing more than companions that share similar interest. However,

ours was one of trust and support, knowing that each would always share the laughter, losses, and tears. Even though

many miles separate us and time has been our enemy, I can still see your smile and I know your mind, sometimes better

than you. You know no words need be said, because no matter what, I understand you.

I really don't understand our crazy friendship. I never really thought about the various magnets that keep us together.

Maybe it's that bond of trust, knowing that our deepest darkest secrets are safe, no matter what. or, maybe it's knowing

that we will always forgive and forget, knowing that each carries their own set of flaws. Or could it be so simple as

knowing that my heart smiles whenever I think about you.

I could go on forever about the times we have shared, good and bad. But, I think the simplest thing to say is, I will

always be their to hold your hand and calm your fears, because together, we are forever friends.

Sam

Dear Linda:

Hi chicky: what's going on in that busy world of yours in Delaware. I hate that you left and went away, but I know you wanted your family. What I don't get is how they are more important than me (ha ha). All I know is that you still have a home here in Charleston and it will be ready for you at anytime.

I do not know what I would have done without you either. As I write to my friends, I realize how lucky I am to have the friends that I have and I will keep you for life. Thank you so much for being there for me throughout this whole ordeal, for I will never forget how wonderful you have been to me. Even though we have not known each other that long, I honestly believe you were put into my life for wonderful reasons. It is always amazing to me when I think of how God works and the things he does. We were brought together when both of us needed someone for so many reasons and I know this will be a life long bond.

As I sit and write these letters please believe me it is so hard. I try not to cry the whole time, but believe me I do. You tell me it is ok to cry sometimes that it is normal, you also tell me I am normal, so I guess I have to start believing you.

I am going to just remember the good times we had when you were here and try not to miss you so much now that you are gone. I know I can talk to you at any time and that is so great. I know I still drive you crazy, but I drive everybody crazy. You know when I miss you most is when I go to the ocean, as many times as we sat at Mariners Cay and watched the Dolphins; it's no wonder.

Please take care of yourself and always remember I am here for you at anytime for anything.

All my love, Cindy Lou Hoo

Dear Cindy~

Fragile thing at times...life, love shattered your world as you'd known it, as you loved it. By your strength and resilience you picked up the brokenness, putting life back together with the pieces you found worth salvaging and discarding those that no longer served you.

Love the pain my friend, accept it if it comes again, and we know it will, because pain is what drives us to change and create something new. So, my friend, savor what life may bring, what it has left behind, and what it will never experience, some things are just not meant to be.

You glow like the sun's reflection through stained glass, your true colors spilling upon this earthly canvas- shades of red; crimson passion waiting to be quenched, the tincture of your inner power and strength prevailing, the pigmented flow of your life's force. The deep blues; of a love lost, hues of serenity flowing through your being bringing peace. Bright greens of spring; a promise of life anew resurrected from the winter of your mourning, buds of new growth blooming into who you have become. Casts of orange; are sunsets- the endings of another day making way for new dawns – the sunrises of hope. Red and blue swirled together creating the purple of your majesty, tinting the regal beauty of your spirit, steadfast against the winds of life. You are a new creation born from your joys and sorrows. Relish your life's colors in this tapestry of your self-portrait.

I always said to you that there was a reason the two of us became friends, I was there to teach you patience and you were there to teach me to move a little faster. Actually, life's experiences have taught you far better than I ever could about patience. You have come a long way, you've worked hard and you have had many who supported you and loved you during this painful but enlightening journey. Life's lessons are meant to be shared, this is how others may benefit from your pain and this book is a little light in the darkness.

I want to share with you a few quotes I've found inspirational when I am facing difficult situations or decisions, hope you find inspiration in them also!

"When you have come to the edge of all that you know and step into the darkness of the unknown, know that one of two things will happen - you will be given something solid to stand on, or you will be taught how to fly."   (~author unknown~)

You are given the gifts of the gods, you create your reality according to you beliefs. Yours is the creative energy that makes your world. There are no limitations to the self except those you *believe* in.   ~ Seth~

~The light within me honors the light within you, my friend. ~
Love,
Linda~

Dear Barry:

What is up? I want to write you a letter and thank you for being such a huge inspiration to me during the worst time of my life. I will never forget the visit at James Island County Park and you convinced me to always just repeat the phrase "I aint got no time for this shit today!" I have said this to myself a least a thousand times a day since then. I also want to thank you for sharing your mom with me at such a difficult time in your lives.

I said in my book how it is amazing how people come back into each others lives at just the right time, well we sure are proof of this! Thank you for sharing your beautiful Lanai friends and family with me. I sure felt safe there and I knew that I would be taken care of no matter what. This was huge in the beginning of my recovery!

I am ending your letter the same as Sharon's and I hope you like it. I know I will never forget these times: Sing with me and smile!

> Whenever I wake up
> Before I put on my make-up
> I say a little prayer for you,
> I'm combing my hair now
> Wondering what dress to wear now
> I say a little prayer for you,
> Forever and ever
> You will be in my heart
> And I will love you,
> There will never be
> Heartbreak for you!

I love you forever, Cindy

What's up chicken butt:

I hope you know that I did not type this letter, but they are my words. It would have taken me 6 months to type it. I just want you to know that I am so glad that your recovery is going well and moving along. It has been a joy to watch you grow and I know that you will overcome this terrible time you have been going through.

I can't wait till pool time again and I am going to be there to help you get over your fear of water that this has left you with. Don't worry we will start slow and I will be there with you ever minute of the way baby girl. I know you love my pool, now let's get in it. The time has come!

Remember my words if you ever get lonely or sad again and always say to yourself "I ain't got no time for this shit today" and "get on with the gettin on". I am so glad that you called me and we got back together again after all those years lost. The Stono days were great, but today is even better.

Keep it cool baby, and I am always here if you need me for anything! Best of luck with your book, I can't wait to read it!

Love ya chick, Barry

My Dearest Hope:

Wow, how we came to be! Just another example of how God knows just what to do at all times. I often sit and ask myself how could Fred have known to put us two together? I can't answer this question, but I sure do thank him every day and love him more for this.

It is so amazing to me how we will continue on our family traditions of keeping the two families together after all these years (the next generation).

As I have watched you grow throughout your illness as I have watched myself, I am amazed at the differences in us. The tears and fears we have shared could have only been shared with someone like you who knew and understood. I want to thank you for all of the times you listened to me and for always being there for me. I don't know if you know how much of a help you have been to me, but believe me you have! I used your faith and strength many times and I thank you for sharing them with me.

As we continue our recovery phase of this horrible illness, I want you to remember one thing and remember it well: God loves you and he wants you to be here to continue to do the things that you do for others. I am watching you get your power back and growing everyday. You are worth it Hope (all you have to do is remember your name).

We are both so lucky to have the wonderful families we have and the support they are giving us. This is priceless and it is something that a lot of people do not have. My one wish in this world is that everyone could have the same as we do and I hope that this wish does come true.

I love you to death and if you do not remember to take your meds every day, I will get on to you (you know I will). It will not be pretty, but it will be necessary. We will get through this and be ourselves again, for this I do know, for God told me so!

I love you, Cindy

Cindy Leopard

March 2009
Dear Cindy:

The Anticipated Therapy Session (2007): Hi, Cindy. Nice to Meet You.
When we met, I didn't know what in the world was going to happen. You
were a wreck. I was a wreck. "What in the 'ham sandwich' was Fred
thinking about?" How could two wreck less people help each other? The
bible says let the blind lead the blind. However, *this is not* the case. God
chose two, very special people to share experiences in order to help others.
He crossed our paths among others to fulfill some predestined purposes or
Kingdom business. Time will tell.

Two Peas In A Pod
This is the beginning of a friendship that will last forever. Even if we have
disagreements, at the end, you will still be my "sister". So here we are, *like*
two peas in a pod. I like peas. Do you like peas? Just kidding around. I
don't want you to think I'm *crazy*. One thing I love about you is the sense of
humor, even when you are not feeling well or good. You are down to earth
and hilarious. ---*Your parents are so cool. I feel welcomed and part of the*
family. You all have got to stop spoiling my child. --- Getting back to you,
helping others is a part of your genuine character. Continue to be who you
are. Continue to be strong. Don't change for anything or anybody.

I'm reserved and quiet. Sometimes too serious. My facial expressions
mislead people. It's just the impressions of early life experiences. Watching
things happen around me and staying out of the way became one of many
survival tactics. I continue to sit back and observe people. Like their
personalities and characters and actions and reactions such as: intentions,
worthiness, trusts, motives, care, concerns, hurts, pains, sufferings, love for
others, selfishness, envy, kindness, helpfulness, and etc. The following
observations are why I have difficulties trusting almost anyone: gossiping
about other people; always negative; snooping around; use people for what
they want; back-stabbing; criticizing other people; spreading false
information; say one thing and do another; being judgmental; and ect., ect.,
ect.. I'd rather find solutions for myself before asking for help. I have trust
issues." Can you be trusted?" I pray for the Lord to correct my defects. Lord
forgive me, help me forgive myself and others.

1

172

Everybody Needs Somebody

I know everybody needs somebody. Why not help each other, rather than make matters worst. Let's find solutions. "Listen everybody, just be sincere and genuine because it makes a huge, huge difference. Treat others the way you want to be treated. It's not what you say, but the way you say it." I know I have defects in my character as well. Constructive criticism makes me a better person. They are welcomed, only to help me be better a person.

My Feelings On Asking for Help

When some people help others, they feel the need to tell the whole world. That's *soooo* not cool. Then when people feel better and try to regain independence, the helpers feel used or unappreciated. Okay, now I feel like I owe debts for their help. Feelings of embarrassment and shame are not healthy.

Ms. Independent: No Thank You. I'll Manage.

It did get to the point to where I needed help. I couldn't help take care of my family or myself. I had to put my pride under the bed and accept help from some people. "I gratefully appreciate your help and support. But, please don't hold this over my head. I never forget those who help me".

Let's take a stroll to the initial unification of our friendship.

Are you ready? Periodically I need to take breaks. Literally I do. My thoughts are going so fast, it's hard to keep up. Wait, wait, wait its scrambling. So please bare with me. I see other things that needs to be done, and forget what I was doing or needed to say. Errr! How frustrating.... Okay I found it. Throughout this letter, comments are made to express my feeling and opinions. Misconceptions, misunderstandings, and ignorance worsen persons with mental problems. My heart aches and I'm just so angry. Forgive me. I may come off as being harsh. But there is a lot of steam I must get off my chest. *This is a part of my road to recovery*. Okay, let's go.

2

The Connection and Reaction

One day at the doctor's office, a suggestion was made to have therapy with
you. We were both a mess, looking like a train wreck. Fatigue, despair, and
weariness displayed themselves all over our bodies (from head to toe). We
planned a trip to the park. The weather was nice and the park was tranquil.
It was hard for you to even walk in the park. By the way, how did we make it
to the park? Several times you called me and said, "Hope, when are we
going to get better. I feel like my head is not attached to my body. The
wiring from my brain is not connecting to my body. They're going separate
ways". Do you remember the place we went that was deeper than Hell? Get
us out of here!!! There is a speck of light at the end of this tunnel. Keep
reaching without a doubt. Even though getting well feels like a never ending
journey, we know deep within ourselves something is keeping us strong. It is
faith, the size of a mustard seed, giving us courage and strength from God.

The Inevitable Happens

Clinical depression among other diagnosis changed my life drastically. I had
symptoms of things I never knew existed. Especially for me. Yeah, Cindy we
know it happens to other people. Not us because we are special. It will skip
us and catch the other people. Our experiences are almost parallel.

Life was spiraling out of control and I hit rock bottom really hard and fast. I
felt and knew something wasn't right. What was it? Predispositions along
with other circumstances pushed me over the edge. Bam!!! Fake it until you
make it was no longer an option. Symptoms such as mood swings, physical
discomfort, and emotional roller coaster rides were surfacing along with other
behaviors. It became evident something terribly was going wrong. In 2007 I
was advised by doctors to take time off from work. Intimidation caused
hesitation to request for leave-time. I had to take care of myself. Explain to
my employer the urgency of taking some weeks off from work. I also stated
to him, "Right now, I am no good to anybody". In the teaching profession,
being sick is not an option. I never thought in a million years I would have to
leave work due to mental conditions. Unfortunately, it led from short-term
leave to sabbatical leave; and then to grieving over the loss of my career. It
turned out to be a BLESSING from God. Everything happens for a reason.
After a decade plus more years on a job, anyone would expect to have a
strong support system from their fellow teachers and administrators and other
staff members.

3

"Thank you so much. Hope you will never get a chance to walk in my shoes". We barely made it second by second, minute by minute, and day by day. Cindy do you think our misunderstood critics could walk in our shoes for a split second? Just a glimpse causes one to gasps and cringe . "Sincerely, I thank those who showed genuine care and support. I greatly appreciate you and may God bless you."

The Denial Stage
This could not be happening to me! Not me! I'm a survivor! I was in complete denial. God is my strength, comfort, joy, Prince of Peace, Lord and Savior, provider, Lover of my soul, and most of all, best friend. Giving up and selfishness were not acceptable. I remember saying all summer long before returning to work, "Lord, if you don't help me, I don't know how I am going to make it. Oh, dear Lord, please help me".

Wow. What a toll it took on me. Cindy, I realized we were not the only ones suffering. It effected everyone around us. At least those who cared or were willing to help us. I'm sure you can relate to the difficulties of expressing your feelings to others. Most of the responses were puzzled looks, negativity, or inconsiderate remarks. How disappointing it was not to have your feelings validated. No one understood what it is like to experience life when it is out control. "Unless you've been there, don't chastise me and discount my feelings when I seek for your attention or help". Someone offended me by saying, "Girl, Hope, I'm tired and stressed. I need to catch a ride with you to Palmetto". If only that person knew what we are going through. Hey Cindy, that rhymes.

I realize now, that a lot of people are not equipped or have the skills to help people like us. It becomes a nuisance to them and the avoiding game begins. Just to have someone listen, without criticism, means a whole lot. A support system is crucial and a necessity to the road of recovery. Most of the time, I sat in the parking lot balling my eyes out with endless tears. There was no place to go. I was so lonely. Cindy, you have a great support system.

Playing the Role
I attempted or pretended (whatever you want to call it) to be as responsible and professional as everybody else. Oh, I'm fine. Everything is lovely. Everything is cool. I have it under control. If they can do it, I can do it too!

4

You know, like I got it going on. I am competent. I have it all together. everything is copestatic. I tried to look and act *normal* to fit in with everybody. What is normal? When you find a normal person please let me know. I need their fingerprints, social security numbers, addresses, phone numbers, and maybe some pictures.

Everybody's brain and body works differently. Some people may hit rock bottom and bounce back up again. Then life goes on for them. Cindy, not in our cases. We need a whole lot of support and coping skills to deal with our lives. We feel each other's pain. You were a critical needs nurse and I was a teacher. The sense of losing our identities is one of the most devastating thing a person could experience. Now where do we fit in?

You Learn Something New Everyday
Sadden to say, no one understands others and us diagnosed with mental disorders. This is a serious life and death illness. Just because it not physically, visible it is no different from other serious conditions. For example as diabetes, cancer, heart disease, and etc. are serious illnesses. Cindy, God may not have forgiven us if we took extreme measures to fix our problems permanently. His will be done. The thought of God and our loved ones kept us alive. They need us and we need us. This is why we must take care of ourselves. Some people are walking around undiagnosed. Most of the their behaviors are evident of serious issues. *They are the crazy ones. We're getting help. Ha ha ha! The joke is on them.* "Don't judge us. You can be one of us too." It can happen to anybody, at anytime. It has no race, gender, profession, or time to whom this may happen." Some people have the nerve of nerves to treat us like we are scum of the earth. We are scorned and looked down. "White collar, blue collar, whoever collar, it pays to treat others with respect. You might need Cindy to be your nurse one day. Due to certain circumstances, people get sick. They may lose skills or knowledge necessary for daily routines. You might need my help to regain knowledge or relearn skills."

The world needs to be educated about mental disorders in order to understand and show compassion for others. Cindy, you are so brave for sharing your personal journey to recovery. Imagine the lives that will be saved and changed.

5

360 Degrees Turn

My phone rang. It was you. A different you. Finally, a new doctor, among others, helped you make a complete turn around. I was so amazed at how well you were doing. Girl you were fired up. Many people, especially prestigious, high position folks will be hearing from you. That's right Cindy go and get them. You are very outspoken and intelligent. Advocating for those with mental diagnosis is priority on your list.

Dumb Things People Say

"Caution! Don't you dare approach anyone with mental problems, and say something stupid. They may attack you. *Not because they are crazy, but because you are ignorant"*. For your sake don't say:
* Snap out of it.
* What's wrong with you?.
* You just want attention.
* Stop crying.
* You are not the only person having problems.
* Get over it.
* Get yourself together.
* You just don't want to work.
* Stop complaining.
* Just pray about it.
* Get up and do something.
* Your lazy.
* You need to get motivated.
We did not choose to be this way. We cry a lot and don't even know why. Who wants to be first in line for a disease or serious illness?"

Cindy, Cindy, Cindy, --- don't they get it already! "Listen people, you can't talk anyone, *diagnosed with a mental disorder*, out of it. It does not work that way. However, your support is gratefully appreciated. Thanks for being so understanding. Thank you for being a good listener. Thank you for not ignoring and dismissing our feelings, *like it can't happen to you*. ect. ect. ect. . . .whatever."

6

Be Gone: Embarrassment, Guilt, and Shame

"What happened to Mrs. Prioleau?" This happened, that happened, everything happened. I must be *real important* for them to try and figure out what happened to me.

Some students, and surprisingly others, recognized me during treatment. How embarrassing for me to be out from a highly, respected, professional job. Well the truth is out. So be it. "If you're here and I'm here, then we all have some things in common. Hello. Now, go tell that."

Cindy you taught me not to be ashamed. You told me this is something we have no control over. We have to try really hard. Medication helps, but we have to do some work too. Who knows? I believe God is using us to help others. We may have fall down, but we will get up and move on. When we fall off the wagon or have set-backs, we'll know exactly what to do.

The Acceptance Stage

The Prayer of Serenity opened my eyes. I often ask myself, "What can I change? What can't I change?" I can change to please myself or change to please other people. Have you ever heard this before? "I like you, but I love me more." I'm working on accepting myself. *What you see is what you get. I am who I who am. First, I must accept it.* . . who cares what anyone thinks!

A big Thanks to My Pea In the Pod

Oh by the way, this letter would not have been written if I did not listen to you. This was a huge task. It was time consuming and required a lot of effort. I did need a little nudge, a little push, and maybe a little reprimanding now and then. You told me, "Take your damn meds!", in so many words.

Thank you for allowing me to express my feelings to you. It's such an honor to be a part of your life. I know much success will follow as you continue to record and share experiences. Anticipation awaits for the book to be released. May God bless everyone's heart to receive this wealth of information. Love and kisses to you Cindy.

7

P.S.
Perfection
"I'm not an editor. So excuse me for any grammatical errors or misspelled words. The spell check did not recognize a particular word. It was not in the dictionary, but I know what I was trying to say. Find the misspelled or nonexistent word. 'You figure it out <u>smart ----------</u>.' Which word is it?"
This is for people who find faults and point out defects of others. Like I said before I'm not perfect.

Teachers are perceived as professionals who have the answers to everything. We are humans too, not walking computers. However we try to do out best. I prayed every morning before going to work, "Lord please bless me with wisdom, knowledge, and understanding to be an effective teacher."

No one is perfect, only God.

Again, thank you. Thank you. Thank you. Thank you. I love you and may continue to bless you!!!

Dear Bonnie:

Hey girl, what's going on today? I know you are typing away for work, and yes thinking about that new beautiful grandbaby of yours. Well I guess I am the last to be a grandma and I must say, yeah! When I sit back and think of the old days, I think you, Marie, and I all turned out to be great mothers, we must have done something right, just look at our children.

I know I didn't see you when I was so sick, but that was my choice. I know you would have been there if I would have let you know how bad it was. I tried really hard to let everyone go on with their lives and not worry about me. But believe me you were thought of a lot.

I am so glad that I am seeing more of you now, for the bitch sessions and coffee times are great. I must say, if there is anyone on this earth that can make me laugh, it is you (I am laughing now just thinking of you)! Let's do it more often now, for you are becoming a great part of my recovery and I thank you so much. We have all been through a lot of good times and bad, but that's ok, for we are all still together.

Luv ya girl, Cindy

Cindy,

Congratulations on finishing your book. It has been so nice reconnecting with you after so many years. Life certainly takes us in many directions, with many obstacles to overcome and you seem to have overcome the most difficult time of your life. The one thing I hope you have learned through your process is that happiness truly comes from within. Another person can heighten your happiness, but truly not be the sole reason for it. I hope your process of healing continues and allows you to get back into the mainstream, working and enjoying life to its fullest potential.

Bonnie

Dear Deb:

Poor Deb, what I have put you through is horrible. When I first got sick and started on all the meds, I must have called you a million times. What a trooper you were and still are. I want to thank you for always taking the time for me and talking to me, no matter how busy you were. You always made me feel better and gave me hope that I would eventually find a med that would work for me. Your encouragement was phenomenal and was a huge help.

I promise you it is ok if you want to call me a pain in the ass, for I know I was. It's nice to know we can laugh about it now, but we sure didn't then. Please know that my trust in you as my pharmacist, my friend, and at one time my mentor, is huge. I loved working with you when I did and what great times we had (I was the lunch girl). I do know one thing, I will never forget how to count to 30. What a team we were!

I can imagine what you were thinking at the time and it must have went like this, "Good grief girl, you are a nurse and I have taught you everything about all these meds, don't you remember anything?" Well believe me that all goes out the window, when it is you that is so sick. I love you as a whole and you have it all. I also thank your wonderful staff, they are all great. Plantation Pharmacy Rocks!   All my love, Cindy

March 21, 2009

I've known Cindy Leopard for 15 years. Maybe longer, but time goes by and dates become unimportant. What is important to me is a transformation that has occurred.

Cindy worked for me as a Pharmacy Technician while she was going to nursing school. She was vivacious, confident with a "no bull shit" type of attitude and determination. Cindy had been divorced from Steve for several years and would talk about how he was the love of her life and how heartbroken she was because they had parted. Over and over again she would talk about him as if he were the greatest man on earth and the question was always asked, "then why the divorce?" One afternoon the phone rang at the Pharmacy and a man asked for Cindy. It was Steve. They hadn't spoken for well over a year and we all wondered if they really were soul mates. The rest is history. They reconciled for awhile, the reasons for the divorce surfaced,and again, Cindy was alone.

Cindy went on to finish her nursing degree and moved on to a job at MUSC. Time passed and as often happens we drifted apart.

In January 2005 I opened my own Pharmacy. Cindy supported the Pharmacy by bringing her business to me and she was happy and successful. She would talk about how she had made the right decision to go into nursing and really loved what she was doing and had met another man who she was head over heels in love with. "Like Steve?" I asked. "Beyond Steve" was her reply. Happy, confident and in love. That was Cindy Leopard's paradise.

Then one day all of that changed. I have never witnessed such a transformation in an individual. Her spirit was completely broken. To this day, I'm not sure if one person can truly cause another's emotional destruction but the Cindy I knew was gone. The woman looked like Cindy, but it was only a shell. She was distraught, housebound, would call me desperate for answers to why she was going through this and I felt totally helpless. She needed professional help, therapy, medication, more help than I could ever give and that made me very sad. I felt sad that I couldn't do more, sad that I didn't have the answers and sad that Cindy couldn't see that. Cindy would call the Pharmacy several times a day and I would answer her questions knowing that the questions were just a front for her need to talk, a need for a lifeline.

Eventually, she did get into therapy. Cindy would still call me several times a day, but now it was to talk about what her Dr. was helping her deal with. There were still questions but now she was hopeful, there was some light and some of the demons had disappeared.

The therapy has definitely made a difference. After one year of being home, she now will come into the Pharmacy with a goal to stay for 15minutes without leaving. Her face will flush and I will assure her that she's ok but sometimes I know she's not ..My hope and prayer is that the old confident, fun loving Cindy will one day return. My gut tells me it will be a long time before that happens. Cindy, from all of us that love you, you have so much to offer your family, your friends and your community. Let us all be your lifeline, let us all celebrate your recovery and let your faith guide you back to a long, healthy, happy life. From our lips to God's ear...

Deb Dapore

Cindy Leopard

Dear William:

I just want to thank you for everything you did for me during my stays at Palmetto. I always knew that when you were there I would be ok. As you know it is not easy being in a place like that, but if you have to be somewhere for safety, that is the place to be.

Thank you for teaching me about my tool box that I know is right under my heart. You gave me the knowledge and God showed me how to work the tools, what a team you both were. I still have my Bible verses you gave me the first time I ever saw you and I will keep them forever.

I don't know if you will ever understand what a huge part you were in my recovery, but I want to tell you that every night when you go to sleep thank yourself for being the wonderful person you are. It brings me great peace to know there are people like you in this world and I will never forget what you have done for me.

God Bless you, Cindy

Dear Robin:

When I wrote about you in my book, I could not use your name, but now I will let everyone know who you are. When you went to Heaven when we were only 23 years old, I never thought a person could ever miss someone so much. As I have grown, I now know that you are still with me everyday and watching over me. I have many angels in Heaven now and you are one of them.

I know that God is with you and you are in the best place in the world, I wonder what it is like up there and I can't wait to see you again. There are many more tasks that God has for me on earth, so it may be many years from now, but that is ok. Our day will come! I just want to let you know that I have never forgotten you for a day and will always miss and love you.

So keep watching over me please, and continue to be with me, for I know that I am with you!

Waiting for our day, Cindy

Dear Peggy:

Hey girl, I see you up there floating on a cloud, drinking a Margarita, and laughing you head off with that huge smile of yours. I just wanted to let you know that I sure do miss that beautiful smile and loud mouth. I always knew you were around ten minutes before I ever saw you, what charm you have.

As you have been watching over me, you know how sick I have been. I want to thank you for being in the lights and showing me the way to God. Your little Anna Marie taught me this! (I said at the beginning of this chapter that it would be a chapter of tears, well I was right, this is very hard)! Please just always remember and do not ever forget that you are in my heart and always will be remembered by me. And yes I know that our day will come when we are together again, after my tasks on earth are done. I can't wait to hear your stories of what you have been up to, for I know they will be fun and exciting.

Keep it fun and groovy up there on those clouds, I know you are, for Heaven must be very colorful with you there. I can't wait to see that beautiful smile again.

I love you, Cindy

Dear Anna Marie:

I know that you are only eleven years old now and you do not remember when you were two. But you did something for me that I will never be able to thank you enough for. When you get older and read this letter you will understand all of this, but now I want you to know that what you did for me helped save my life. I talked about what you did in the book, so I will no go into it again, but I do want you to know that my lamp is still on my kitchen counter and I still talk to God every night.

It is such an honor watching you grow up and I am sorry that I have missed the last two years of your life, but I am coming back some now and I hope to never leave you again.

When you grow up and read this book, I want you to thank yourself for being such an important part of my recovery and always love yourself. You are blessed with such a beautiful family and are a very lucky young lady. I will always feel as though you are one of mine and love you with all my heart! Thanks Anna!

I love you, Aunt Cindy

MY ROUGH PATCH

You can't see it, you can't touch it,
but you know it's there, cause you can feel it.
It has a force greater than all others, it's the only
thing that can keep you down so deep
in the hole, where it is so dark and cold.
It doesn't allow for company,
for loneliness is it's purpose, it's the control
that wants to keep you, the control that only it can have.
What can be so strong, that can take our souls from us,
that can take our lives from us, and keep us for so long?
If only God could fix it, or having faith could forbid it,
or doing good could never allow it!
But then we would never have the privilege of
learning courage, strength, and confidence,
for this is our gift from above!
(December, 2007)

Well I have written to you my heart, my soul and my guts, I have even shared my poems that I do not know how to write. There is only one more thing I can do and that is sing you a song, please remember when you sing this song, I am singing it with you:

I'M ALIVE (Title of Song)

When you call on me

When I hear you breathe

When you look at me

I can touch the sky

When you bless the day

I just drift away

God knows that I'm Alive

Writer Unknown

Performed by Celine Dion

As I would ride around during my recovery, I would find sayings on church boards and other places. I took pictures of these boards on my cell phone and I want to share some of them with you. *How so few words can say so much!*

ATM Inside
Acceptance
Truth
Mercy

Give yourself
Permission to heal!

Peace is not the
Absence of conflict
But the ability to
Cope with it

Imagine being
Really happy!

Want the change?
Be inspired by the
flame!

You can't heal
What you won't feel!

There is a remedy and
His name is Jesus
Christ!

Stretch your mind,
Open your heart!

Jesus the original
Christmas Gift!

EPILOGUE

As I finally get to the end of my book I would like to tell you about my life today. In three months it will be two years since I became so sick and lost all hope for life. I never in my life time thought that I would want to die and leave all of my loved ones and friends behind; *but I did*.

Today I am still under the care of Dr. Z. and my recovery is going well. I still have fears of water (the shower), going out in public and sleeping. The panic that I suffered is very debilitating and stops all aspects of your life. I am able to go to friends houses now and stay for a little while, have a cup of coffee and visit. How long I can stay depends on how quiet things are and how my medications are affecting me on that day. I try every day to get out and go a few places to help my recovery and retrain my brain that this is normal for me to do. I use all my tools: faith, strength, and courage as hard as I can and believe me they do help. I do know that I love life and I can laugh again and yes, I do love that I am alive! Yes, I do cry sometimes still when I get sad, but I know now that this a normal emotion. It is ok to cry when things upset me, but I can stop the tears and make them positive. Huge step!

I do sit sometimes and wonder what my future will bring; will I ever be completely well; will I ever be a nurse again; will I ever be able to just put this all behind me and live a normal life as I did before; will I ever be capable of falling in love again? I do ask myself these questions all the time, but I must just make myself believe every day that "Yes all the answers will be yes."

My only hope is that my experiences can help many people to understand that they can go through a time like this and get better. I have all the faith in the world that my life will be back to normal again one day and this is what keeps me working so hard on my recovery. I know that I have said this before, but I am going to say it again, "*Please do not be ashamed of this kind of illness, for it can happen to anyone at any time and you must get the proper help for a good recovery.*" I thank God every day for all the support that I have had from my wonderful family, doctors, and friends that I have been blessed with. I would have never made it without them.

I would like to thank everyone for all the great letters that were written to me in the last chapter. This quickly became my favorite chapter and I hope you enjoy them. As you can see, everything can turn out ok and I do know that my life: "*WILL BE A DANCE AGAIN.*"

God Bless you all!

The End

Printed in the United States
by Baker & Taylor Publisher Services